D1455562

The Tent Dwellers

by Albert Bigelow Paine

Author of "The Van Dwellers," "The Lucky Piece," etc.

Originally published in 1908.

Chapter One

Come, shape your plans where the fire is bright,

And the shimmering glasses are—

When the woods are white in the winter's night,

Under the northern star.

It was during the holiday week that Eddie proposed the matter. That is Eddie's way. No date, for him, is too far ahead to begin to plan anything that has vari-colored flies in it, and tents, and the prospect of the campfire smell. The very mention of these things will make his hair bristle up (rather straight, still hair it is and silvered over with premature wisdom) and put a new glare into his spectacles (rather wide, round spectacles they are) until he looks even more like an anarchist than usual—more indeed than in the old Heidelberg days, when, as a matter of truth, he is a gentle soul; sometimes, when he has transgressed, or thinks he has, almost humble.

As I was saying, it was during the holidays—about the end of the week, as I remember it—and I was writing some letters at the club in the little raised corner that looks out on the park, when I happened to glance down toward the fireplace, and saw Eddie sitting as nearly on his coat collar as possible, in one of the wide chairs, and as nearly in the open hickory fire as he could get, pawing over a book of Silver Doctors, Brown Hackles and the like, and dreaming a long, long dream.

Now, I confess there is something about a book of trout flies, even at the year's end, when all the brooks are flint and gorged with white, when all the north country hides under seamless raiment that stretches even to the Pole itself—even at such a time, I say, there is something about those bits of gimp, and gut, and feathers, and steel, that prick up the red blood of any man—or of any woman, for that matter—who has ever flung one of those gaudy things into a swirl of dark water, and felt the swift, savage tug on the line and heard the music of the singing reel.

I forgot that I was writing letters and went over there.

"Tell me about it, Eddie," I said. "Where are you going, this time?"

Then he unfolded to me a marvelous plan. It was a place in Nova Scotia—he had been there once before, only, this time he was going a different route, farther into the wilderness, the deep unknown, somewhere even the guides had never been. Perhaps stray logmen had been there, or the Indians; sportsmen never. There had been no complete surveys, even by the government. Certain rivers were known by their outlets, certain lakes by name. It was likely that they formed the usual network and that the circuit could be made by water, with occasional carries. Unquestionably the waters swarmed with trout. A certain imaginative Indian, supposed to have penetrated the unknown, had declared that at one place were trout the size of one's leg.

Eddie became excited as he talked and his hair bristled. He set down a list of the waters so far as known, the names of certain guides, a number of articles of provision and an array of camp paraphernalia. Finally he made maps and other drawings and began to add figures. It was dusk when we got back. The lights were winking along the park over the way, and somewhere through the night, across a waste of cold, lay the land we had visited, still waiting to be explored. We wandered out into the dining room and settled the matter across a table. When we rose from it, I was pledged—pledged for June; and this was still December, the tail of the old year.

Chapter Two

And let us buy for the days of spring,

While yet the north winds blow!

For half the joy of the trip, my boy,

Is getting your traps to go.

Immediately we, that is to say, Eddie, began to buy things.
It is Eddie's way to read text-books and to consult
catalogues with a view of making a variety of purchases.
He has had a great deal of experience in the matter of camp
life, but being a modest man he has a fund of respect for the
experience of others. Any one who has had enough ability,
or time, to write a book on the subject, and enough
perseverance, or money, to get it published, can preach the
gospel of the woods to Eddie in the matter of camp
appointments; and even the manufacturers' catalogues are
considered sound reading. As a result, he has accumulated
an amazing collection of articles, adapted to every time and
season, to every change of wind and temperature, to every
spot where the tent gleams white in the campfire's blaze,
from Greenland's icy mountains to India's coral strand. Far
be it from me to deride or deprecate this tendency, even
though it were a ruling passion. There are days, and nights,
too, recalled now with only a heart full of gratitude because
of Eddie's almost inexhaustible storehouse of comforts for
soul and flesh—the direct result of those text-books and
those catalogues, and of the wild, sweet joy he always

found in making lists and laying in supplies. Not having a turn that way, myself, he had but small respect for my ideas of woodcraft and laid down the law of the forest to me with a firm hand. When I hinted that I should need a new lancewood rod, he promptly annulled the thought. When I suggested that I might aspire as far as a rather good split bamboo, of a light but serviceable kind, he dispelled the ambition forthwith.

"You want a noibwood," he said. "I have just ordered one, and I will take you to the same place to get it."

I had never heard of this particular variety of timber, and it seemed that Eddie had never heard of it, either, except in a catalogue and from the lips of a dealer who had imported a considerable amount of the material. Yet I went along, meekly enough, and ordered under his direction. I also selected an assortment of flies—the prettiest he would let me buy. A few others which I had set my heart on I had the dealer slip in when Eddie wasn't looking. I was about to buy a curious thing which a trout could not come near without fatal results, when the wide glare of his spectacles rested on me and my courage failed. Then he selected for me a long landing net, for use in the canoe, and another with an elastic loop to go about the neck, for wading; leaders and leader-boxes and the other elementary necessaries of angling in the northern woods. Of course such things were as A, B, C to Eddie. He had them in infinite variety, but it was a field day and he bought more. We were out of the place at last, and I was heaving a sigh of relief that this part of it was over and I need give the matter no further thought, when Eddie remarked:

"Well, we've made a pretty good start. We can come down here a lot of times between now and June."

"But what for?" I asked.

"Oh, for things. You haven't a sleeping bag yet, and we'll be thinking of other stuff right along. We can stay over a day in Boston, too, and get some things there. I always do that. You want a good many things. You can't get them in the woods, you know."

Eddie was right about having plenty of time, for this was January. He was wrong, however, about being unable to get things in the woods. I did, often. I got Eddie's.

Chapter Three

Now the gorges break and the streamlets wake

And the sap begins to flow,

And each green bud that stirs my blood

Is a summons, and I must go.

Eddie could not wait until June. When the earliest April buds became tiny, pale-green beads—that green which is like the green of no other substance or season—along certain gray branches in the park across the way, when there was a hint and flavor of stirring life in the morning sun, then there came a new bristle into Eddie's hair, a new gleam into his glasses, and I felt that the wood gods were calling, and that he must obey.

"It is proper that one of us should go on ahead," he argued, "and be arranging for guides, canoes and the like at the other end."

I urged that it was too soon—that the North was still white and hard with cold—that preliminaries could be arranged by letter. I finally suggested that there were still many things he would want to buy. He wavered then, but it was no use. Eddie can put on a dinner dress with the best and he has dined with kings. But he is a cave-, a cliff- and a tree-dweller in his soul and the gods of his ancestors were not to be gainsaid. He must be on the ground, he declared, and as for the additional articles we might need, he would send me lists. Of course, I knew he would do that, just as I knew that the one and mighty reason for his going was to be where he could smell the first breath of the budding North and catch the first flash and gleam of the waking trout in the nearby waters.

He was off, then, and the lists came as promised. I employed a sort of general purchasing agent at length to attend to them, though this I dared not confess, for to Eddie it would have been a sacrilege not easy to forgive. That I could delegate to another any of the precious pleasure of preparation, and reduce the sacred functions of securing certain brands of eating chocolate, camp candles, and boot grease (three kinds) to a commercial basis, would, I felt, be a thing almost impossible to explain. The final list, he notified me, would be mailed to a hotel in Boston, for the reason, he said, that it contained things nowhere else procurable; though I am convinced that a greater reason was a conviction on his part that no trip could be complete without buying a few articles in Boston at the last hour before sailing, and his desire for me to experience this concluding touch of the joy of preparation. Yet I was glad, on the whole, for I was able to buy secretly some things he never would have permitted—among them a phantom minnow which looked like a tin whistle, a little four-ounce bamboo rod, and a gorgeous Jock Scott fly with two hooks. The tin whistle and the Jock Scott looked deadly, and the rod seemed adapted to a certain repose of muscle after a period of activity with the noibwood. I decided to conceal these purchases about my person and use them when Eddie wasn't looking.

But then it was sailing time, and as the short-nosed energetic steamer dropped away from the dock, a storm (there had been none for weeks before) set in, and we pitched and rolled, and through a dim disordered night I clung to my berth and groaned, and stared at my things in the corner and hated them according to my condition. Then morning brought quiet waters and the custom house at Yarmouth, where the tourist who is bringing in money, and maybe a few other things, is made duly welcome and not bothered with a lot of irrelevant questions. What Nova Scotia most needs is money, and the fisherman and the hunter, once through the custom house, become a greater source of revenue than any tax that could be laid on their modest, not to say paltry, baggage, even though the contents of one's trunk be the result of a list such as only Eddie can prepare. There is a wholesome restaurant at Yarmouth, too, just by the dock, where after a tossing night at sea one welcomes a breakfast of good salt ham, with eggs, and pie—two kinds of the latter, pumpkin and mince.

I had always wondered where the pie-belt went, after it reached Boston. Now I know that it extends across to Yarmouth and so continues up through Nova Scotia to Halifax. Certain New Englanders more than a hundred years ago, "went down to Nova Scotia," for the reason that they fostered a deeper affection for George, the King, than for George of the Cherry Tree and Hatchet. The cherry limb became too vigorous in their old homes and the hatchet too sharp, so they crossed over and took the end of the pie-belt along. They maintained their general habits and speech, too, which in Nova Scotia to-day are almost identical with those of New England. But I digress—a grave and besetting sin.

I had hoped Eddie would welcome me at the railway station after the long forenoon's ride—rather lonely, in spite of the new land and the fact that I made the acquaintance of a fisherman who taught me how to put wrappings on a rod. Eddie did not meet me. He sent the wagon, instead, and I enjoyed a fifteen-mile ride across June hills where apple blossoms were white, with glimpses of lake and stream here and there; through woods that were a promise of the wilderness to come; by fields so thickly studded with bowlders that one to plant them must use drill and dynamite, getting my first impression of the interior of Nova Scotia alone. Then at last came a church, a scattering string of houses, a vista of lakes, a neat white hotel and the edge of the wilderness had been reached. On the hotel steps a curious, hairy, wild-looking figure was capering about doing a sort of savage dance—perhaps as a preparation for war. At first I made it out to be a counterpart of pictures I had seen of Robinson Crusoe on his desert island. Then I discovered that it wore wide spectacles and these in the fading sunlight sent forth a familiar glare. So it was Eddie, after all, and no edged tool had touched hair or beard since April. I understood, now, why he had not met me at the station.

Chapter Four

Now, the day is at hand, prepare, prepare—

Make ready the boots and creel,

And the rod so new and the fly-book, too,

The line and the singing reel.

Eddie's room and contents, with Eddie in the midst of them, was a marvel and a revelation. All the accouterments of former expeditions of whatever sort, all that he had bought for this one, all that I had shipped from week to week, were gathered there. There were wading boots and camp boots and moccasins and Dutch bed-slippers and shoepacks—the last-named a sort of Micmac Indian cross between a shoe and a moccasin, much affected by guides, who keep them saturated with oil and wear them in the water and out— there were nets of various sizes and sorts, from large minnow nets through a line of landing nets to some silk head nets, invented and made by Eddie himself, one for each of us, to pull on day or night when the insect pests were bad. There was a quantity of self-prepared ointment, too, for the same purpose, while of sovereign remedies, balms and anodynes for ills and misfortunes, Eddie's collection was as the sands of the sea. Soothing lotions there were for wounds new and old; easing draughts for pains internal and external; magic salves such as were used by the knights of old romance, Amadis de Gaul and others,

for the instant cure of ghastly lacerations made by man or
beast, and a large fresh bottle of a collodion preparation
with which the victim could be painted locally or in
general, and stand forth at last, good as new—restored,
body, bones and skin. In addition there was a certain bottle
of the fluid extract of gelsemium, or something like that,
which was recommended for anything that the rest of the
assortment could do, combined. It was said to be good for
everything from a sore throat to a snake bite—the list of its
benefits being recorded in a text-book by which Eddie set
great store.

"Take it, by all means, Eddie," I said, "then you won't need
any of the others."

That settled it. The gelsemium was left behind.

I was interested in Eddie's rods, leaning here and there on
various parcels about the room. I found that the new
noibwood, such as I had ordered, was only a unit in a very
respectable aggregate—rather an unimportant unit it
appeared by this time, for Eddie calmly assured me that the
tip had remained set after landing a rather small trout in a
nearby stream and that he did not consider the wood
altogether suitable for trout rods. Whereupon I was moved
to confess the little bamboo stick I had bought in Boston,
and produced it for inspection. I could see that Eddie
bristled a bit as I uncased it and I think viewed it and
wiggled it with rather small respect. Still, he did not
condemn it utterly and I had an impulse to confess the other
things, the impossible little scale-wing flies, the tin whistle
and the Jock Scott with two hooks. However, it did not
seem just the psychological moment, and I refrained.

As for Eddie's flies, viewed together, they were a dazzling lot. There were books and books of them—American, English, Scotch and what not. There was one book of English dry-flies, procured during a recent sojourn abroad, to be tried in American waters. One does not dance and jiggle a dry-fly to give it the appearance of life—of some unusual creature with rainbow wings and the ability to wriggle upstream, even against a swift current. The dry-fly is built to resemble life itself, color, shape and all, and is cast on a slow-moving stream where a trout is seen to rise, and allowed to drift with the gently flowing current exactly over the magic spot. All this Eddie explained to me and let me hold the book a little time, though I could see he did not intend to let me use one of the precious things, and would prefer that I did not touch them.

He was packing now and I wandered idly about this uncatalogued museum of sporting goods. There was a heap of canvas and blankets in one corner—a sleeping bag, it proved, with an infinite number of compartments, or layers; there were hats of many shapes, vests of many fabrics, coats of many colors. There were things I had seen before only in sporting goods windows; there were things I had never seen before, anywhere; there were things of which I could not even guess the use. In the center of everything were bags—canvas and oil-skin receptacles, vigorously named "tackle bag," "wardrobe," "war bag" and the like—and into these the contents of the room were gradually but firmly disappearing, taking their pre-destined place according to Eddie's method—for, after all, it was a method—and as I looked at Eddie, unshaven for weeks, grizzled and glaring, yet glowing with deep kindliness and the joy of anticipation, I could think of nothing but Santa Claus, packing for his annual journey that magic bag which holds more and ever more, and is so deep and so wide in its beneficence that after all the comforts and the sweets of life are crowded within, there still is room for more a-top. Remembering my own one small bag which I had planned to take, with side pockets for tackle, and a place between for certain changes of raiment, I felt my unimportance more and more, and the great need of having an outfit like Eddie's—of having it in the party, I mean, handy like, where it would be easy to get hold of in time of need. I foresaw that clothes would want mending; also, perhaps, rods; and it was pleasant to note that my tent-mate would have boxes of tools for all such repairs.

I foresaw, too, that I should burn, and bruise, and cut myself and that Eddie's liniments and lotions and New Skin would come in handy. It seemed to me that in those bags would be almost everything that human heart could need or human ills require, and when we went below where Del and Charlie, our appointed guides, were crowding certain other bags full of the bulkier stores—packages, cans and bottles, and when I gazed about on still other things—tents, boots, and baskets of camp furniture—I had a sense of being cared for, though I could not but wonder how two small canoes were going to float all that provender and plunder and four strong men.

Chapter Five

Then away to the heart of the deep unknown,

Where the trout and the wild moose are—

Where the fire burns bright, and tent gleams white

Under the northern star.

It was possible to put our canoes into one of the lakes near the hotel and enter the wilderness by water—the Liverpool chain—but it was decided to load boats and baggage into wagons and drive through the woods—a distance of some seventeen uneven miles—striking at once for the true wilderness where the larger trout were said to dwell and the "over Sunday" fisherman does not penetrate. Then for a day or two we would follow waters and portages familiar to our guides, after which we would be on the borders of the unknown, prepared to conquer the wilderness with an assortment of fishing rods, a supply of mosquito ointment and a pair of twenty-two caliber rifles, these being our only guns.

It seems hardly necessary to say that we expected to do little shooting. In the first place it was out of season for most things, though this did not matter so much, for Eddie had in some manner armed himself with a commission from the British Museum to procure specimens dead or alive, and this amounted to a permit to kill, and skin, and hence to eat, promiscuously and at will. But I believe as a party, we were averse to promiscuous killing; besides it is well to be rather nice in the matter of special permits. Also, we had come, in the main, for trout and exploration. It was agreed between us that, even if it were possible to hit anything with our guns, we would not kill without skinning, and we wouldn't skin without eating, after which resolution the forest things probably breathed easier, for it was a fairly safe handicap.

I shall not soon forget that morning drive to Jake's Landing, at the head of Lake Kedgeemakoogee, where we put in our canoes. My trip on the train along the coast, and the drive through farming country, more or less fertile, had given me little conception of this sinister land—rock-strewn and barren, seared by a hundred forest fires. Whatever of green timber still stands is likely to be little more than brush. Above it rise the bare, gaunt skeletons of dead forests, bleached with age, yet blackened by the tongues of flame that burned out the life and wealth of a land which is now little more than waste and desolation—the haunt of the moose, the loon and the porcupine, the natural home of the wild trout.

It is true, that long ago, heavy timber was cut from these woods, but the wealth thus obtained was as nothing to that which has gone up in conflagrations, started by the careless lumbermen and prospectors and hunters of a later day. Such timber as is left barely pays for the cutting, and old sluices are blocked and old dams falling to decay. No tiller of the soil can exist in these woods, for the ground is heaped and drifted and windrowed with slabs and bowlders, suggesting the wreck of some mighty war of the gods—some titanic missile-flinging combat, with this as the battle ground.

Bleak, unsightly, unproductive, mangled and distorted out of all shape and form of loveliness, yet with a fierce, wild fascination in it that amounts almost to beauty—that is the Nova Scotia woods.

Only the water is not like that. Once on the stream or lake and all is changed. For the shores are green; the river or brook is clear and cold—and tarry black in the deep places; the water leaps and dashes in whirlpools and torrents, and the lakes are fairy lakes, full of green islands—mere ledges, many of them, with two or three curious sentinel pines— and everywhere the same clear, black water, and always the trout, the wonderful, wild, abounding Nova Scotia trout.

To Jake's Landing was a hard, jolting drive over a bad road, with only a break here and there where there is a house or two, and maybe a sawmill and a post-office, the last sentinels of civilization. It was at Maitland, the most important of these way stations, that we met Loon. Maitland is almost a village, an old settlement, in fact, with a store or two, some pretty houses and a mill. Loon is a dog of the hound variety who makes his home there, and a dear and faithful friend of Eddie's, by the latter's account. Indeed, as we drew near Maitland, after announcing that he would wish to stop at the Maitland stores to procure some new things he had thought of, Eddie became really boastful of an earlier friendship with Loon. He had met Loon on a former visit, during his (Loon's) puppyhood days, and he had recorded the meeting in his diary, wherein Loon had been set down as "a most intelligent and affectionate young dog." He produced the diary now as evidence, and I could see that our guides were impressed by this method of systematic and absolute record which no one dare dispute. He proceeded to tell us all he knew about Loon, and how glad Loon would be to see him again, until we were all jealous that no intelligent and affectionate hound dog was waiting for us at Maitland to sound the joy of welcome and to speed us with his parting bark.

Then all at once we were at Maitland and before Loon's home, and sure enough there in the front yard, wagging both body and tail, stood Loon. It took but one glance for Eddie to recognize him. Perhaps it took no more than that for Loon to recognize Eddie. I don't know; but what he did was this: He lifted up his voice as one mourning for a lost soul and uttered such a series of wails and lamentations as only a hound dog in the deepest sorrow can make manifest.

"Wow-ow-oo-ow-wow-oo-oo-o."

The loon bird sends a fairly unhappy note floating down the wet, chill loneliness of a far, rainy lake, but never can the most forlorn of loons hope to approach his canine namesake of Maitland. Once more he broke out into a burst of long-drawn misery, then suddenly took off under the house as if he had that moment remembered an appointment there, and feared he would be late. But presently he looked out, fearfully enough, and with his eyes fixed straight on Eddie, set up still another of those heart-breaking protests.

As for Eddie, I could see that he was hurt. He climbed miserably down from the wagon and crept gently toward the sorrowing hound.

"Nice Loon—nice, good Loon. Don't you remember me?"

"Wow-ow-oo-ow-wow-oo-oo-o," followed by another disappearance under the house.

"Come, Loon, come out and see your old friend—that's a good dog!"

It was no use. Loon's sorrow would not be allayed, and far beyond Maitland we still heard him wailing it down the wind.

Of course it was but natural that we should discuss the matter with Eddie. He had assured us that dogs never forget, and we pressed him now to confess what extreme cruelty or deceit he had practiced upon Loon in his puppyhood, that the grown hound dog had remembered, and reproached him for to-day. But for the most part Eddie remained silent and seemed depressed. Neither did he again produce his diary, though we urged him to do so, in order that he might once more read to us what he had recorded of Loon. Perhaps something had been overlooked, something that would make Loon's lamentations clear. I think we were all glad when at last there came a gleam through the trees and we were at Jake's Landing, where our boats would first touch the water, where we would break our bread in the wilderness for the first time.

It was not much of a place to camp. There was little shade, a good deal of mud, and the sun was burning hot. There was a remnant of black flies, too, and an advance guard of mosquitoes. Eddie produced his jug of fly mixture and we anointed ourselves for the first time, putting on a pungent fragrance which was to continue a part of us, body and bone, so long as the wilderness remained our shelter. It was greasy and sticky and I could not muster an instant liking for the combined fragrance of camphor, pennyroyal and tar. But Eddie assured me that I would learn to love it, and I was willing to try.

I was more interested in the loading of the canoes. Del, stout of muscle and figure—not to say fat, at least not over fat—and Charlie, light of weight and heart—sometimes known as Charles the Strong—were packing and fitting our plunder into place, condensing it into a tight and solid compass in the center of our canoes in a way that commanded my respect and even awe. I could see, however, that when our craft was loaded the water line and the gunwale were not so far apart, and I realized that one would want to sit decently still in a craft like that, especially in rough water.

Meantime, Eddie had coupled up a rod and standing on a projecting log was making a few casts. I assumed that he was merely giving us an exhibition of his skill in throwing a fly, with no expectation of really getting a rise in this open, disturbed place. It was fine, though, to see his deft handling of the rod and I confess I watched him with something of envy. I may confess, too, that my own experience with fly casting had been confined to tumbling brooks with small pools and overhanging boughs, where to throw a fly means merely to drop it on a riffle, or at most to swing it out over a swirling current below a fall. I wondered as I watched Eddie if I ever should be able to send a fly sailing backward and then shoot it out forward a matter of twenty yards or so with that almost imperceptible effort of the wrist; and even if I did learn the movement, if I could manage to make the fly look real enough in such smooth, open water as this to fool even the blindest and silliest of trout.

But, suddenly, where Eddie's fly—it was a Silver Doctor, I think—fell lightly on the water, there was a quick swirl, a flash and then a widening circle of rings.

"You got him comin'," commented Charlie, who, it seems, had been noticing.

The fly went skimming out over the water again and softly as thistle seed settled exactly in the center of the circling rings. But before it touched, almost, there came the flash and break again, and this time there followed the quick stiffening of the rod, a sudden tightening of the line, and a sharp, keen singing of the reel.

"That's the time," commented Charlie and reached for a landing net.

To him it was as nothing—a thing to be done a hundred times a day. But to me the world heaved and reeled with excitement. It was the first trout of the expedition, the first trout I had ever seen taken in such water, probably the largest trout I had ever seen taken in any water. In the tension of the moment I held my breath, or uttered involuntary comments.

It was beautiful to see Eddie handle that trout. The water was open and smooth and there is no gainsaying Eddie's skill. Had he been giving an exhibition performance it could not have been more perfect. There was no eagerness, no driving and dragging, no wild fear of the fish getting away. The curved rod, the taut swaying line, and the sensitive hand and wrist did the work. Now and again there was a rush, and the reel sang as it gave line, but there was never the least bit of slack in the recover. Nearer and nearer came the still unseen captive, and then presently our fisherman took the net from his guide, there was a little dipping movement in the water at his feet and the first trout of the expedition was a visible fact—his golden belly and scarlet markings the subject of admiration and comment.

It was not a very big fish by Nova Scotia standards—about three-quarters of a pound, I believe; but it was the largest trout I had ever seen alive, at that time, and I was consumed with envy. I was also rash. A little more, and I had a rod up, was out on a log engaged in a faithful effort to swing that rod exactly like Eddie's and to land the fly precisely in the same place.

But for some reason the gear wouldn't work. In front of me, the fly fell everywhere but in the desired spot, and back of me the guides dodged and got behind bushes. You see, a number three steel hook sailing about promiscuously in the air, even when partially concealed in a fancy bunch of feathers, is a thing to be avoided. I had a clear field in no time, but perhaps Eddie had caught the only fish in the pool, for even he could get no more rises. Still I persisted and got hot and fierce, and when I looked at Eddie I hated him because he didn't cut his hair, and reflected bitterly that it was no wonder a half-savage creature like that could fish. Finally I hooked a tree top behind me and in jerking the fly loose made a misstep and went up to my waist in water. The tension broke then—I helped to break it—and the fishing trip had properly begun.

The wagons had left us now, and we were alone with our canoes and our guides. Del, the stout, who was to have my especial fortunes in hand, knelt in the stern of the larger canoe and I gingerly entered the bow. Then Eddie and his guide found their respective places in the lighter craft and we were ready to move. A moment more and we would drop down the stream to the lake, and so set out on our long journey.

I recall now that I was hot and wet and still a little cross. I had never had any especial enthusiasm about the expedition

and more than once had regretted my pledge made across
the table at the end of the old year. Even the bustle of
preparation and the journey into a strange land had only
mildly stirred me, and I felt now that for me, at least, things
were likely to drag. There were many duties at home that
required attention. These woods were full of mosquitoes,
probably malaria. It was possible that I should take cold, be
very ill and catch no fish whatever. But then suddenly we
dropped out into the lake Kedgeemakoogee, the lake of the
fairies—a broad expanse of black water, dotted with green
islands, and billowing white in the afternoon wind, and just
as we rounded I felt a sudden tug at the end of my line
which was trailing out behind the canoe.

In an instant I was alive. Del cautioned me softly from the
stern, for there is no guide who does not wish his charge to
acquit himself well.

"Easy now—easy," he said. "That's a good one—don't
hurry him."

But every nerve in me began to tingle—every drop of blood
to move faster. I was eaten with a wild desire to drag my
prize into the boat before he could escape. Then all at once
it seemed to me that my line must be fast, the pull was so
strong and fixed. But looking out behind, Del saw the water
break just then—a sort of double flash.

"Good, you've got a pair," he said. "Careful, now, and we'll
save 'em both."

To tell the truth I had no hope of saving either, and if I was
careful I didn't feel so. When I let the line go out, as I was
obliged to, now and then, to keep from breaking it
altogether, I had a wild, hopeless feeling that I could never

take it up again and that the prize was just that much farther away. Whenever there came a sudden slackening I was sickened with a fear that the fish were gone, and ground the reel handle feverishly. Fifty yards away the other canoe, with Eddie in the bow, had struck nothing as yet, and if I could land these two I should be one ahead on the score. It seems now a puny ambition, but it was vital then. I was no longer cold, or hot, or afraid of malaria, or mosquitoes, or anything of the sort. Duties more or less important at home were forgotten. I was concerned only with those two trout that had fastened to my flies, the Silver Doctor and the Parmcheenie Belle, out there in the black, tossing water, and with the proper method of keeping my line taut, but not too taut, easy, but not too easy, with working the prize little by little within reach of the net. Eddie, suddenly seeing my employment, called across congratulations and encouragement. Then, immediately, he was busy too, with a fish of his own, and the sport, the great, splendid sport of the far north woods, had really begun.

I brought my catch near the boatside at last, but it is no trifling matter to get two trout into a net when they are strung out on a six-foot leader, with the big trout on the top fly. Reason dictates that the end trout should go in first and at least twice I had him in, when the big fellow at the top gave a kick that landed both outside. It's a mercy I did not lose both, but at last with a lucky hitch they were duly netted, in the canoe, and I was weak and hysterical, but triumphant. There was one of nearly a pound and a half, and the other a strong half-pound, not guess weight, but by Eddie's scales, which I confess I thought niggardly. Never had I taken such fish in the Adirondack or Berkshire streams I had known, and what was more, these were two at a time! [1]

Eddie had landed a fine trout also, and we drew alongside, now, for consultation. The wind had freshened, the waves were running higher, and with our heavy canoes the six-mile paddle across would be a risky undertaking. Why not pitch our first night's camp nearby, here on Jim Charles point—a beautiful spot where once long ago a half-civilized Indian had made his home? In this cove before dark we could do abundant fishing.

For me there was no other plan. I was all enthusiasm, now. There were trout here and I could catch them. That was enough. Civilization—the world, flesh and the devil—mankind and all the duties of life were as nothing. Here were the woods and the waters. There was the point for the campfire and the tents. About us were the leaping trout. The spell of the forest and the chase gripped me body and soul. Only these things were worth while. Nothing else mattered—nothing else existed.

We landed and in a little while the tents were white on the shore, Del and Charlie getting them up as if by conjury. Then once more we were out in the canoes and the curved rod and the taut line and the singing reel dominated every other force under the wide sky. It was not the truest sport, maybe, for the fish were chiefly taken with trolling flies. But to me, then, it did not matter. Suffice it that they were fine and plentiful, and that I was two ahead of Eddie when at last we drew in for supper.

That was joy enough, and then such trout—for there are no trout on earth like those one catches himself—such a campfire, such a cozy tent (Eddie's it was, from one of the catalogues), with the guides' tent facing, and the fire between. For us there was no world beyond that circle of light that on one side glinted among boughs of spruce and cedar and maple and birch, and on the other, gleamed out on the black water. Lying back on our beds and smoking, and looking at the fire and the smoke curling up among the dark branches toward the stars, and remembering the afternoon's sport and all the other afternoons and mornings and nights still to come, I was moved with a deep sense of gratitude in my heart toward Eddie.

"Eddie," I murmured, "I forgive you all those lists, and everything, even your hair. I begin to understand now something of how you feel about the woods and the water, and all. Next time——"

Then (for it was the proper moment) I confessed fully—the purchasing agent, the tin whistle, even the Jock Scott with two hooks.

Chapter Six

Nearer the fire the shadows creep—

The brands burn dim and red—

While the pillow of sleep lies soft and deep

Under a weary head.

When one has been accustomed to the comforts of civilized
life—the small ones, I mean, for they are the only ones that
count—the beginning of a wild, free life near to nature's
heart begets a series of impressions quite new, and
strange—so strange. It is not that one misses a house of
solid walls and roof, with stairways and steam radiators.
These are the larger comforts and are more than made up
for by the sheltering temple of the trees, the blazing
campfire and the stairway leading to the stars. But there are
things that one does miss—a little—just at first. When we
had finished our first evening's smoke and the campfire was
burning low—when there was nothing further to do but go
to bed, I suddenly realized that the man who said he would
be willing to do without all the rest of a house if he could
keep the bathroom, spoke as one with an inspired
knowledge of human needs.

I would not suggest that I am a person given to luxurious
habits and vain details in the matter of evening toilet. But
there are so many things one is in the habit of doing just

about bedtime, which in a bathroom, with its varied small conveniences, seem nothing at all, yet which assume undue proportions in the deep, dim heart of nature where only the large primitive comforts have been provided. I had never been in the habit, for instance, of stumbling through several rods of bushes and tangled vines to get to a wash-bowl that was four miles wide and six miles long and full of islands and trout, and maybe snapping turtles (I know there were snapping turtles, for Charlie had been afraid to leave his shoepacks on the beach for fear the turtles would carry them off), and I had not for many years known what it was to bathe my face on a ground level or to brush my teeth in the attitude of prayer. It was all new and strange, as I have said, and there was no hot water—not even a faucet—that didn't run, maybe, because the man upstairs was using it. There wasn't any upstairs except the treetops and the sky, though, after all, these made up for a good deal, for the treetops feathered up and faded into the dusky blue, and the blue was sown with stars that were caught up and multiplied by every tiny wrinkle on the surface of the great black bowl and sent in myriad twinklings to our feet.

Still, I would have exchanged the stars for a few minutes, for a one-candle power electric light, or even for a single gas jet with such gas as one gets when the companies combine and establish a uniform rate. I had mislaid my tube of dentifrice and in the dim, pale starlight I pawed around and murmured to myself a good while before I finally called Eddie to help me.

"Oh, let it go," he said. "It'll be there for you in the morning. I always leave mine, and my soap and towel, too."

He threw his towel over a limb, laid his soap on a log and faced toward the camp. I hesitated. I was unused to leaving

my things out overnight. My custom was to hang my towel
neatly over a rack, to stand my toothbrush upright in a glass
on a little shelf with the dentifrice beside it. Habit is strong.
I did not immediately consent to this wide and gaudy
freedom of the woods.

"Suppose it rains," I said.

"All the better—it will wash the towels."

"But they will be wet in the morning."

"Um—yes—in the woods things generally are wet in the
morning. You'll get used to that."

It is likewise my habit to comb my hair before retiring, and
to look at myself in the glass, meantime. This may be due
to vanity. It may be a sort of general inspection to see if I
have added any new features, or lost any of those plucked
from the family tree. Perhaps it is only to observe what the
day's burdens have done for me in the way of wrinkles and
gray hairs. Never mind the reason, it is a habit; but I didn't
realize how precious it was to me until I got back to the
tent and found that our only mirror was in Eddie's
collection, set in the back of a combination comb-brush
affair about the size of one's thumb.

Of course it was not at all adequate for anything like a
general inspection. It would just about hold one eye, or a
part of a mouth, or a section of a nose, or a piece of an ear
or a little patch of hair, and it kept you busy guessing where
that patch was located. Furthermore, as the comb was a part
of the combination, the little mirror was obliged to be
twinkling around over one's head at the precise moment
when it should have been reflecting some portion of one's

features. It served no useful purpose, thus, and was not much better when I looked up another comb and tried to use it in the natural way. Held close and far off, twisted and turned, it was no better. I felt lost and disturbed, as one always does when suddenly deprived of the exercise of an old and dear habit, and I began to make mental notes of some things I should bring on the next trip.

There was still a good deal to do—still a number of small but precious conveniences to be found wanting. Eddie noticed that I was getting into action and said he would stay outside while I was stowing myself away; which was good of him, for I needed the room. When I began to take on things I found I needed his bed, too, to put them on. I suppose I had expected there would be places to hang them. I am said to be rather absent-minded, and I believe I stood for several minutes with some sort of a garment in my hand, turning thoughtfully one way and another, probably expecting a hook to come drifting somewhere within reach. Yes, hooks are one of the small priceless conveniences, and under-the-bed is another. I never suspected that the space under the bed could be a luxury until I began to look for a place to put my shoes and handbag. Our tent was just long enough for our sleeping-bags, and just about wide enough for them—one along each side, with a narrow footway between. They were laid on canvas stretchers which had poles through wide hems down the sides—the ends of these poles (cut at each camp and selected for strength and springiness) spread apart and tacked to larger cross poles, which arrangement raised us just clear of the ground, leaving no space for anything of consequence underneath. You could hardly put a fishing rod there, or a pipe, without discomfort to the flesh and danger to the articles. Undressing and bestowing oneself in an upper berth is attended with problems, but the berth is not so narrow, and it is flat and solid, and there are hooks and little hammocks and things—valuable advantages, now fondly recalled. I finally piled everything on Eddie's bed, temporarily. I didn't know what I was going to do with it next, but anything was a boon for the moment. Just then Eddie looked in.

"That's your pillow material, you know," he said, pointing to my medley of garments. "You want a pillow, don't you?"

Sure enough, I had no pillow, and I did want one. I always want a pillow and a high one. It is another habit.

"Let me show you," he said.

So he took my shoes and placed them, one on each side of my couch, about where a pillow should be, with the soles out, making each serve as a sort of retaining wall. Then he began to double and fold and fill the hollow between, taking the bunchy, seamy things first and topping off with the softer, smoother garments in a deft, workmanlike way. I was even moved to add other things from my bag to make it higher and smoother.

"Now, put your bag on the cross-pole behind your pillow and let it lean back against the tent. It will stay there and make a sort of head to your bed, besides being handy in case you want to get at it in the night."

Why, it was as simple and easy as nothing. My admiration for Eddie grew. I said I would get into my couch at once in order that he might distribute himself likewise.

But this was not so easy. I had never got into a sleeping-bag before, and it is a thing that requires a little practice to do it with skill and grace. It has to be done section at a time, and one's night garment must be worked down co-ordinately in order that it may not become merely a stuffy life-preserver thing under one's arms. To a beginner this is slow, warm work. By the time I was properly down among the coarse, new blankets and had permeated the remotest corners of the clinging envelope, I had had a lot of hard exercise and was hot and thirsty. So Del brought me a drink of water. I wasn't used to being waited on in that way, but it was pleasant. After all there were some conveniences of camp life that were worth while. And the bed was comfortable and the pillow felt good. I lay watching Eddie shape his things about, all his bags and trappings falling naturally into the places they were to occupy through the coming weeks. The flat-topped bag with the apothecary stores and other urgency articles went at the upper end of the little footway, and made a sort of table between our beds. Another bag went behind his pillow, which he made as he had made mine, though he topped it off with a little rubber affair which he inflated while I made another mental memorandum for next year. A third bag——

But I did not see the fate of the third bag. A haze drifted in between me and the busy little figure that was placing and pulling and folding and arranging—humming a soothing ditty meantime—and I was swept up bodily into a cloud of sleep.

Chapter Seven

Now, Dawn her gray green mantle weaves

To the lilt of a low refrain—

The drip, drip, drip of the lush green leaves

After a night of rain.

The night was fairly uneventful. Once I imagined I heard something smelling around the camp, and I remember having a sleepy curiosity as to the size and manner of the beast, and whether he meant to eat us and where he would be likely to begin. I may say, too, that I found some difficulty in turning over in my sleeping-bag, and that it did rain. I don't know what hour it was when I was awakened by the soft thudding drops just above my nose, but I remember that I was glad, for there had been fires in the woods, and the streams were said to be low. I satisfied myself that Eddie's patent, guaranteed perfectly waterproof tent was not leaking unduly, and wriggling into a new position, slept.

It was dull daylight when I awoke. Through the slit in the tent I could see the rain drizzling on the dead campfire. Eddie—long a guest of the forest lost now in the multiple folds of his sleeping-bag—had not stirred. A glimpse of the guides' tent opposite revealed that the flap was still tightly drawn. There was no voice or stir of any living creature.

Only the feet of the rain went padding among the leaves
and over the tent.

Now, I am not especially given to lying in bed, and on this
particular morning any such inclination was rather less
manifest than usual. I wanted to spread myself out, to be
able to move my arms away from my body, to whirl around
and twist and revolve a bit without so much careful
preparation and deliberate movement.

Yet there was very little to encourage one to get up. Our
campfire—so late a glory and an inspiration—had become
a remnant of black ends and soggy ash. I was not overhot
as I lay, and I had a conviction that I should be less so
outside the sleeping-bag, provided always that I could
extricate myself from that somewhat clinging, confining
envelope. Neither was there any immediate prospect of
breakfast—nobody to talk to—no place to go. I had an
impulse to arouse Eddie for the former purpose, but there
was something about that heap of canvas and blankets
across the way that looked dangerous. I had never seen him
roused in his forest lair, and I suspected that he would be
savage. I concluded to proceed cautiously—in some
manner which might lead him to believe that the fall of a
drifting leaf or the note of a bird had been his summons. I
worked one arm free, and reaching out for one of my
shoes—a delicate affair, with the soles filled with splices
for clambering over the rocks—I tossed it as neatly as
possible at the irregular bunch opposite, aiming a trifle
high. It fell with a solid, sickening thud, and I shrank down
into my bag, expecting an eruption. None came. Then I was
seized with the fear that I had killed or maimed Eddie. It
seemed necessary to investigate.

I took better aim this time and let go with the other shoe.

"Eddie!" I yelled, "are you dead?"

There was a stir this time and a deep growl. It seemed to take the form of words, at length, and I caught, or fancied I did, the query as to what time it was; whereupon I laboriously fished up my watch and announced in clear tones that the hand was upon the stroke of six. Also that it was high time for children of the forest to bestir themselves.

At this there was another and a deeper growl, ending with a single syllable of ominous sound. I could not be sure, but heard through the folds of a sleeping-bag, the word sounded a good deal like hell and I had a dim conviction that he was sending me there, perhaps realizing that I was cold. Then he became unconscious again, and I had no more shoes.

Yet my efforts had not been without effect. There was a nondescript stir in the guides' tent, and presently the head of Charles, sometimes called the Strong, protruded a little and was withdrawn. Then that of Del, the Stout, appeared and a little later two extraordinary semi-amphibious figures issued—wordless and still rocking a little with sleep—and with that deliberate precision born of long experience went drabbling after fuel and water that the morning fire might kindle and the morning pot be made to boil.

They were clad in oilskins, and the drapery of Charles deserves special attention. It is likely that its original color had been a flaunt of yellow, and that it had been bedizened with certain buttonholes and hems and selvages and things, such as adorn garments in a general way of whatever nature or sex. That must have been a long time ago. It is improbable that the oldest living inhabitant would be able to testify concerning these items.

Observing him thoughtfully as he bent over the wet ashes and skillfully cut and split and presently brought to flame the little heap of wood he had garnered, there grew upon me a realization of the vast service that suit of oilskins must have rendered to its owners—of the countless storms that had beaten upon it; of the untold fires that had been kindled under its protection; of the dark, wild nights when it had served in fording torrents and in clambering over slippery rocks, indeed of all the ages of wear and tear that had eaten into its seams and selvages and hues since the day when Noah first brought it out of the Ark and started it down through the several generations which had ended with our faithful Charles, the Strong.

I suppose this is just one of those profitless reflections which is likely to come along when one is still tangled up in a sleeping-bag, watching the tiny flame that grows a little brighter and bigger each moment and forces at last a glow of comfort into the tent until the day, after all, seems worth beginning, though the impulse to begin it is likely to have diminished. I have known men, awake for a long time, who have gone on to sleep during just such morning speculations, when the flames grew bright and brighter and crackled up through the little heap of dry branches and sent that glow of luxury into the tent. I remember seeing our guide adjust a stick at an angle above the fire, whereby to suspend a kettle, and men, suddenly, of being startled from somewhere—I was at the club, I think, in the midst of a game of pool—by a wild whoop and the spectacle of Eddie, standing upright in the little runway between our beds, howling that the proper moment for bathing had arrived, and kicking up what seemed to me a great and unnecessary stir.

The idea of bathing on such a morning and in that primitive costume had not, I think, occurred to me before, but I saw presently there was nothing else for it. A little later I was following Eddie, cringing from the cold, pelting rain, limping gingerly over sharp sticks and pebbles to the water's edge. The lake was shallow near the shore which meant a fearful period of wading before taking the baptismal plunge that would restore one's general equilibrium. It required courage, too, for the water was icy—courage to wade out to the place, and once there, to make the plunge. I should never have done it if Eddie had not insisted that according to the standard text-books the day in every well-ordered camp always began with this ceremony. Not to take the morning dip, he said, was to manifest a sad lack of the true camping spirit. Thus prodded, I bade the world a hasty good-by and headed for the bottom. A moment later we were splashing and puffing like seals, shouting with the fierce, delightful torture of it— wide awake enough now, and marvelously invigorated when all was over.

We were off after breakfast—a breakfast of trout and flapjacks—the latter with maple sirup in the little eating tent. The flapjacks were Del's manufacture, and his manner of tossing the final large one into the air and catching it in the skillet as it fell, compelled admiration.

The lake was fairly smooth and the rain no longer fell. A gray morning—the surface of the water gray—a gray mantle around the more distant of the islands, with here and there sharp rocks rising just above the depths. It was all familiar enough to the guides, but to me it was a new world. Seated in the bow I swung my paddle joyously, and even with our weighty load it seemed that we barely touched the water. One must look out for the rocks, though, for a sharp point plunged through the bottom of a canoe might mean shipwreck. A few yards away, Eddie and his guide—light-weight bodies, both of them—kept abreast, their appearance somehow suggesting two grasshoppers on a straw.

It is six miles across Kedgeemakoogee and during the passage it rained. When we were about half-way over I felt a drop or two strike me and saw the water about the canoe spring up into little soldiers. A moment later we were struck on every side and the water soldiers were dancing in a multitude. Then they mingled and rushed together. The green islands were blotted out. The gates of the sky swung wide.

Of course it was necessary to readjust matters. Del drew on his oilskins and I reached for my own. I had a short coat, a sou'wester, and a pair of heavy brown waders, so tall that they came up under my arms when fully adjusted. There was no special difficulty in getting on the hat and coat, but to put on a pair of waders like that in the front end of a canoe in a pouring rain is no light matter. There seemed no good place to straighten my legs out in order to get a proper pull. To stand up was to court destruction, and when I made an attempt to put a leg over the side of the canoe Del admonished me fearfully that another such move would send us to the bottom forthwith. Once my thumbs pulled out of the straps and I tumbled back on the stores, the rain beating down in my face. I suppose the suddenness of the movement disturbed the balance of the boat somewhat, for Del let out a yell that awoke a far-away loon, who replied dismally. When at last I had the feet on, I could not get the tops in place, for of course there was no way to get them anywhere near where they really belonged without standing up. So I had to remain in that half-on and half-off condition, far from comfortable, but more or less immune to wet. I realized what a sight I must look, and I could hardly blame Eddie for howling in derision at me when he drew near enough to distinguish my outline through the downpour. I also realized what a poor rig I had on for swimming, in event of our really capsizing, and I sat straight and still and paddled hard for the other side.

It was not what might be termed a "prolonged and continuous downpour." The gray veil lifted from the islands. The myriad of battling soldiers diminished. Presently only a corporal's guard was leaping and dancing about the canoe. Then these disappeared. The clouds broke away. The sun came. Ahead of us was a green shore—the other side of Kedgeemakoogee had been reached.

Chapter Eight

Where the trail leads back from the water's edge—

Tangled and overgrown—

Shoulder your load and strike the road

Into the deep unknown.

We were at the beginning of our first carry, now—a stretch of about two miles through the woods. The canoes were quickly unloaded, and as I looked more carefully at the various bags and baskets of supplies, I realized that they were constructed with a view of being connected with a man's back. I had heard and read a good deal about portages and I realized in a general way that the canoes had to be carried from one water system to another, but somehow I had never considered the baggage. Naturally I did not expect it to get over of its own accord, and when I came to consider the matter I realized that a man's back was about the only place where it could ride handily and with reasonable safety. I also realized that a guide's life is not altogether a holiday excursion.

I felt sorry for the guides. I even suggested to Eddie that he carry a good many of the things. I pointed out that most of them were really his, anyway, and that it was too bad to make our faithful retainers lug a drug store and sporting goods establishment, besides the greater part of a provision warehouse. Eddie sympathized with the guides, too. He was really quite pathetic in his compassion for them, but he didn't carry any of the things. That is, any of those things.

It is the etiquette of portage—of Nova Scotia portage, at least—that the fisherman shall carry his own sporting paraphernalia—which is to say, his rods, his gun, if he has one, his fishing basket and his landing net. Also, perhaps, any convenient bag of tackle or apparel when not too great an inconvenience. It is the business of the guides to transport the canoes, the general outfit, and the stores. As this was to be rather a long carry, and as more than one trip would be necessary, it was proposed to make a half-way station for luncheon, at a point where a brook cut the trail.

But our procession did not move immediately. In the first place one of the canoes appeared to have sprung a leak, and after our six-mile paddle this seemed a proper opportunity to rest and repair damages. The bark craft was hauled out, a small fire scraped together and the pitch pot heated while the guides pawed and squinted about the boat's bottom to find the perforation. Meantime I tried a few casts in the lake, from a slanting rock, and finally slipped in, as was my custom. Then we found that we did not wish to wait until reaching the half-way brook before having at least a bite and sup. It was marshy and weedy where we were and no inviting place to serve food, but we were tolerably wet, and we had paddled a good way. We got out a can of corned beef and a loaf of bread, and stood around in the ooze, and cut off chunks and chewed and gulped and worked them down into place. Then we said we were ready, and began to load up. I experimented by hanging such things as landing nets and a rod-bag on my various projections while my hands were to be occupied with my gun and a tackle-bag. The things were not especially heavy, but they were shifty.

I foresaw that the rod-bag would work around under my arm and get in the way of my feet, and that the landing nets would complicate matters. I tied them all in a solid bunch at last, with the gun inside. This simplified the problem a good deal, and was an arrangement for which I had reason to be thankful.

It was interesting to see our guides load up. Charles, the Strong, had been well named. He swung a huge basket on his back, his arms through straps somewhat like those which support an evening gown, and a-top of this, other paraphernalia was piled. I have seen pack burros in Mexico that were lost sight of under their many burdens and I remembered them now, as our guides stood forth ready to move. I still felt sorry for them (the guides, of course) and suggested once more to Eddie that he should assume some of their burdens. In fact, I was almost willing to do so myself, and when at the last moment both Charlie and Del stooped and took bundles in each hand, I was really on the very point of offering to carry something, only there was nothing more to carry but the canoes, and of course they had to be left for the next trip. I was glad, though, of the generous impulse on my part. There is always comfort in such things. Eddie and I set out ahead.

There is something fine and inspiring about a portage. In the first place, it is likely to be through a deep wood, over a trail not altogether easy to follow. Then there is the fascinating thought that you are cutting loose another link from everyday mankind—pushing a chapter deeper into the wilderness, where only the more adventurous ever come. Also, there is the romantic gipsy feeling of having one's possessions in such compass that not only the supplies themselves, but the very means of transportation may be bodily lifted and borne from one water link to another of that chain which leads back ever farther into the unknown.

I have suggested that a portage trail is not always easy to follow. As a matter of fact the chances are that it will seldom be easy to follow. It will seldom be a path fit for human beings. It won't be even a decent moose path, and a moose can go anywhere that a bird can. A carry is meant to be the shortest distance between two given places and it doesn't strive for luxury. It will go under and over logs, through scratchy thickets and gardens of poison ivy. It will plow through swamps and quicksands; it will descend into pits; it will skin along the sharp edge of slippery rocks set up at impossible angles, so that only a mountain goat can follow it without risking his neck. I believe it would climb a tree if a big one stood directly in its path.

We did not get through with entire safety. The guides, shod in their shoepacks, trained to the business, went along safely enough, though they lurched a good deal under their heavy cargoes and seemed always on the verge of disaster. Eddie and I did not escape. I saw Eddie slip, and I heard him come down with a grunt which I suspected meant damage. It proved a serious mishap, for it was to one of his reels, a bad business so early in the game. I fell, too, but I only lost some small areas of skin which I knew Eddie would replace with joy from a bottle in his apothecary bag.

But there were things to be seen on that two-mile carry. A partridge flew up and whirred away into the bushes. A hermit thrush was calling from the greenery, and by slipping through very carefully we managed to get a sight of his dark, brown body. Then suddenly Eddie called to me to look, and I found him pointing up into a tree.

"Porky, Porky!" he was saying, by which I guessed he had found a porcupine, for I had been apprised of the numbers in these woods. "Come, here's a shot for you," he added, as I drew nearer. "Porcupines damage a lot of trees and should be killed."

I gazed up and distinguished a black bunch clinging to the body of a fairly large spruce, near the top. "He doesn't seem to be damaging that tree much," I said.

"No, but he will. They kill ever so many. The State of Maine pays a bounty for their scalps."

I looked up again. Porky seemed to be inoffensive enough, and my killing blood was not much aroused.

"But the hunters and logmen destroy a good many more trees with their fires," I argued. "Why doesn't the State of Maine and the Province of Nova Scotia pay a bounty for the scalps of a few hunters and logmen?"

But Eddie was insistent. It was in the line of duty, he urged, to destroy porcupines. They were of no value, except, perhaps, to eat.

"Will you agree to eat this one if I shoot him?" I asked, unbundling my rifle somewhat reluctantly.

"Of course—that's understood."

I think even then I would have spared Porky's life, but at that moment he ran a little way up the tree. There was something about that slight movement that stirred the old savage in me. I threw my rifle to my shoulder, and with hasty aim fired into the center of the black bunch.

I saw it make a quick, quivering jump, slip a little, and cling fast. There was no stopping now. A steady aim at the black ball this time, and a second shot, followed by another convulsive start, a long slide, then a heavy thudding fall at our feet—a writhing and a twisting—a moaning and grieving as of a stricken child.

And it was not so easy to stop this. I sent shot after shot into the quivering black, pin-cushioned ball before it was finally still—its stained, beautifully pointed quills scattered all about. When it was over, I said:

"Well, Eddie, they may eat up the whole of Nova Scotia, if they want to—woods, islands and all, but I'll never shoot another, unless I'm starving."

We had none of us starved enough to eat that porcupine. In the first place he had to be skinned, and there seemed no good place to begin. The guides, when they came up, informed us that it was easy enough to do when you knew how, and that the Indians knew how and considered porcupine a great delicacy. But we were not Indians, at least not in the ethnological sense, and the delicacy in this instance applied only to our appetites. I could see that Eddie was anxious to break his vow, now that his victim was really dead by my hand. We gathered up a few of the quills—gingerly, for a porcupine quill once in the flesh, is said to work its way to the heart—and passed on, leaving the black pin cushion lying where it fell. Perhaps Porky's death saved one or two more trees for the next Nova Scotia fire.

There were no trout for luncheon at our half-way halt. The brook there was a mere rivulet, and we had not kept the single small fish caught that morning. Still I did not mind.

Not that I was tired of trout so soon, but I began to suspect that it would require nerve and resolution to tackle them three times a day for a period of weeks, and that it might be just as well to start rather gradually, working in other things from time to time.

I protested, however, when Del produced a can of Columbia River salmon. That, I said, was a gross insult to every fish in the Nova Scotia waters. Canned salmon on a fishing trip! The very thought of it was an offense; I demanded that it be left behind with the porcupine. Never, I declared, would I bemean myself by eating that cheap article of commerce—that universally indigenous fish food—here in the home of the chief, the prince, the ne plus ultra of all fishes—the Nova Scotia trout.

So Del put the can away, smiling a little, and produced beans. That was different. One may eat beans anywhere under the wide sky.

Chapter Nine

The black rock juts on the hidden pool

And the waters are dim and deep,

Oh, lightly tread—'tis a royal bed,

And a king lies there asleep.

It was well into the afternoon before the canoes reached the end of the carry—poking out through the green—one on the shoulders of each guide, inverted like long shields, such as an ancient race might have used as a protection from arrows. Eddie and I, meantime, had been employed getting a mess of frogs, for it was swampy just there, and frogs, mosquitoes and midges possessed the locality. We anointed for the mosquitoes and "no-see-ums," as the midges are called by the Indians, and used our little rifles on the frogs.

I wonder, by the way, what mosquitoes were made for. Other people have wondered that before, but you can't overdo the thing. Maybe if we keep on wondering we shall find out. Knowledge begins that way, and it will take a lot of speculation to solve the mosquito mystery.

I can't think of anything that I could do without easier than the mosquito. He seems to me a creature wholly devoid of virtues. He is a glutton, a poisoner, a spreader of disease, a dispenser of disturbing music. That last is the hardest to forgive. If he would only be still I could overlook the other things. I wonder if he will take his voice with him into the next world. I should like to know, too, which place he is bound for. I should like to know, so I could take the other road. [2]

Across Mountain Lake was not far, and then followed another short carry—another link of removal—to a larger lake, Pescawess. It was nearly five miles across Pescawess, but we made good time, for there was a fair wind. Also we had the knowledge that Pescawah Brook flows in on the other side, and the trout there were said to be large and not often disturbed.

We camped a little below this brook, and while the tents were going up Eddie and I took one of the canoes and slipped away past an island or two, among the strewn bowlders at the stream's mouth, pausing to cast a little here and there, though at first with no other result than to get our lines in a mess together.

"Now, say, old man," Eddie began, as my line made a turn around his neck and a half-dozen twists around his tackle, the whole dropping in a heap in the water, "you mustn't cast like that. You should use the treetop cast—straight up in the air, when there's a man behind you. Don't you know you might lacerate a fellow's ear, or put a hook through his lip, or his nose, or something?"

I said that I was sorry, and that if he would give me a few points on the treetop cast, and then avoid sitting in the treetops as much as possible himself I thought there would be no further danger.

He was not altogether pacified. The lines were in a bad tangle and he said it was wasting precious time to be fooling that way. Clearly two men could not fish from one canoe and preserve their friendship, and after our lines were duly parted and Eddie had scolded me sufficiently, we went ashore just below where the swift current tumbles in, and made our way to the wide, deep, rock-bound pools above. The going was pretty thick and scratchy, and one had to move deliberately.

Eddie had more things to carry than I did, for he had brought his gun and his long-handled net, and these, with his rod, set up and properly geared with a long leader and two flies, worried him a good deal. The net had a way of getting hung on twigs. The line and leader displayed a genius for twisting around small but tough branches and vines, the hooks caught in unexpected places, and the gun was possessed to get between his legs. When I had time to consider him, he was swearing steadily and I think still blaming me for most of his troubles, though the saints know I was innocent enough and not without difficulties of my own. Chiefly, I was trying to avoid poison ivy, which is my bane and seemed plentiful in this particular neck of the woods.

We were out at last, and the wide, dark pool, enclosed by great black bowlders and sloping slabs of stone, seemed as if it might repay our efforts. Not for years, maybe, had an artificial fly been cast in that water. Perhaps Eddie was still annoyed with me, for he pushed farther up to other pools, and was presently lost to view.

I was not sorry of this, for it may be remembered that I had thus far never caught a trout by casting in open, smooth water, and I was willing to practice a little alone. I decided to work deliberately, without haste and excitement, and to get my flies caught in the treetops as infrequently as possible. I adjusted them now, took a good look behind and tossed my cast toward the other side of the dark pool. I thought I did it rather well, too, and I dragged the flies with a twitching motion, as I had seen Eddie do it, but nothing happened. If there were trout anywhere in the world, they would be in a pool like this, and if there was ever an evening for them it was now. It was in the nature of probability that Eddie would come back with a good string, and I could not let him find me a confessed failure. So once more I sent the flies out over the pool—a little farther this time, and twitched them a little more carefully, but I might have been fishing in a tub, so far as any tangible fish were concerned.

A little more line and a reckless back cast landed my tail fly in a limb—a combination which required time and patience to disengage. By the time I had worked out the puzzle it began to seem like a warm evening. Then I snapped the flies into several different corners of the pool, got hung again on the same limb, jerked and broke the fly and repeated some of the words I had learned from Eddie as we came through the brush.

I was cooler after that, and decided to put on a new and different fly. I thought a Jenny Lind would be about the thing, and pretty soon was slapping it about—at first hopefully, then rashly. Then in mere desperation I changed the top fly and put on a Montreal. Of course I wouldn't catch anything. I never would catch anything, except by trolling, as any other duffer, or even a baby might, but I would have fun with the flies, anyway. So the Montreal went capering out over the pool, landing somewhere amid the rocks on the other side. And then all at once I had my

hands full of business, for there was a leap and a splash,
and a z-z-z-t of the reel, and a second later my rod was
curved like a buggy whip, the line as taut as wire and
weaving and swaying from side to side with a live, heavy
body, the body of a trout—a real trout—hooked by me with
a fly, cast on a quiet pool.

I wouldn't have lost that fish for money. But I was deadly
afraid of doing so. A good thing for me, then, my practice
in landing, of the evening before. "Easy, now—easy," I said
to myself, just as Del had done. "If you lose this fish you're
a duffer, sure enough; also a chump and several other
undesirable things. Don't hurry him—don't give him
unnecessary line in this close place where there may be
snags—don't, above all things, let him get any slack on
you. Just a little line, now—a few inches will do—and keep
the tip of your rod up. If you point it at him and he gets a
straight pull he will jump off, sure, or he will rush and you
cannot gather the slack. Work him toward you, now,
toward your feet, close in—your net has a short handle, and
is suspended around your neck by a rubber cord. The cord
will stretch, of course, but you can never reach him over
there. Don't mind the reel—you have taken up enough line.
You can't lift out a fish like that on a four-ounce rod—on
any rod short of a hickory sapling. Work him toward you,
you gump! Bring your rod up straighter—straighter—
straight! Now for the net—carefully—oh, you clumsy
duffer, to miss him! Don't you know that you can't thrash
him into the net like that?—that you must dip the net under
him? I suppose you thought you were catching mice. You
deserve to lose him altogether. Once more, now, he's right
at your feet—a king!"

Two long backward steps after that dip, for I must be
certain that he was away from the water's edge. Then I

bumped into something—something soft that laughed. It was Eddie, and he had two fish in his landing net.

"Bully!" he said. "You did it first-rate, only you don't need to try to beat him to death with the landing net. Better than mine," he added, as I took my trout off the fly. "Suppose now we go below. I've taken a look and there's a great pool, right where the brook comes out. We can get to it in the canoe. I'll handle the canoe while you fish."

That, also, is Eddie's way. He had scolded me and he would make amends. He had already taken down his rod, and we made our way back through the brush without much difficulty, though I was still hot with effort and excitement, and I fear a little careless about the poison ivy. A few minutes later, Eddie, who handles a canoe—as he does everything else pertaining to the woods—with grace and skill, had worked our craft among the rocks into the wide, swift water that came out from under a huge fallen log— the mouth of Pescawah Brook.

"Cast there," he said, pointing to a spot just below the log.

Within twenty minutes from that time I had learned more about fishing—real trout fishing—than I had known before in all my life. I had, in Eddie, a peerless instructor, and I had such water for a drill ground as is not found in every day's, or every week's, or every month's travel. Besides, there were fish. Singly and in pairs they came—great, beautiful, mottled fellows—sometimes leaping clear of the water like a porpoise, to catch the fly before it fell. There were none less than a pound, and many over that weight. When we had enough for supper and breakfast—a dozen, maybe—we put back the others that came, as soon as taken from the hook. The fishing soon ended then, for I believe the trout have some means of communication, and one or two trout returned to a pool will temporarily discourage the others. It did not matter. I had had enough, and once more, thanks to Eddie, returned to the camp, jubilant.

Chapter Ten

Where the path is thick and the branches twine

I pray you, friend, beware!

For the noxious breath of a lurking vine

May wither your gladness there.

It was raining next morning, but that was not the worst. During the night I had awakened with a curious, but not entirely unfamiliar sensation about one of my eyes. There was a slight irritant, itching tendency, and the flesh felt puffy to the touch. I tried to believe it was imagination, and went to sleep again.

But there was no doubt next morning. Imagination is a taunting jade, but I don't believe she could close one of my eyes and fatten up the other—not in so short a time. It was poison ivy—that was what it was—and I had it bad.

When Eddie woke, which he did, finally, he took one look at me and dove back into his sleeping bag out of pure fear. He said I was a sight, and he was correct. Our one looking-glass was not big enough to hold all of even one eye, but taking my features in sections I could see that he had not overstated my appearance. Perhaps the situation was amusing, too—at least Eddie, and even the guides, professed to be entertained—but for me, huddled against one side of a six by eight tent—a tent otherwise packed with bags and bundles and traps of various kinds—Eddie's things, mostly, and Eddie himself among them—with a chill rain coming down outside, and with a face swollen and aching in a desperate way with poison, the quality of the humor to me seemed strained when I tried to distinguish it with the part of an eye I had left.

Eddie meantime had dived down into his bag of remedies, happy to have a chance to use any or all of them, and was laying them out on his sleeping bag in front of him—in his lap, as it were, for he had not yet arisen—reading the labels and wondering which he should try on me first. I waited a little, then I said:

"Never mind those, Eddie, give me your alcohol and witch hazel."

But then came an embarrassing moment. Running his eye over the bottles and cans Eddie was obliged to confess that not one of them contained either alcohol or witch hazel.

"Eddie," I said reproachfully, "can it be, in a drug store like that, there is neither alcohol nor witch hazel?"

He nodded dismally.

"I meant to bring them," he said, "but the triple extract of gelsemium would do such a lot of things, and I thought I didn't need them, and then you made fun of that, and— and——"

"Never mind, Eddie," I said, "I have an inspiration. If alcohol cures it, maybe whisky will, and thank Heaven we did bring the whisky!"

We remained two days in that camp and I followed up the whisky treatment faithfully. It rained most of the time, so the delay did not matter. Indeed it was great luck that we were not held longer by that distressing disorder which comes of the malignant three-leaved plant known as mercury, or poison ivy. Often it has disqualified me for a week or more. But the whisky treatment was a success. Many times a day I bathed my face in the pure waters of the lake and then with the spirits—rye or Scotch, as happened to be handy. By the afternoon of the first day I could see to put sirup on my flapjacks, and once between showers I felt able to go out with Eddie in the canoe, during which excursion he took a wonderful string of trout in a stagnant-looking, scummy pool where no one would ever expect trout to lie, and where no one but Eddie could have taken them at all.

By the next morning, after a night of sorrow—for my face always pained and itched worse when everybody was in bed and still, with nothing to soothe me but the eternal drip, drip from the boughs and from the eaves of the tent—the swelling was still further reduced, and I felt able to travel. And I wish to add here in all seriousness that whatever may be your scruples against the use of liquors, don't go into the woods without whisky—rye or Scotch, according to preference. Alcohol, of course, is good for poison ivy, but whisky is better. Maybe it is because of the drugs that wicked men are said to put into it. Besides, whisky has other uses. The guides told us of one perfectly rigid person who, when he had discovered that whisky was being included in his camp supplies, had become properly incensed, and commanded that it be left at home. The guides had pleaded that he need not drink any of it, that they would attend to that part of what seemed to them a necessary camp duty, but he was petrified in his morals, and the whisky remained behind.

Well, they struck a chilly snap, and it rained. It was none of your little summer landscape rains, either. It was a deadly cold, driving, drenching saturation. Men who had built their houses on the sand, and had no whisky, were in a bad fix. The waves rose and the tents blew down, and the rigid, fossilized person had to be carried across an overflowed place on the back of a guide, lifting up his voice meanwhile in an effort to convince the Almighty that it was a mistake to let it rain at this particular time, and calling for whisky at every step.

It is well to carry one's morals into the woods, but if I had to leave either behind, I should take the whisky.

It was a short carry to Lake Pescawah. Beyond that water we carried again about a quarter of a mile to a lake called Pebbleloggitch—perhaps for the reason that the Indian who picked out the name couldn't find a harder one. From Pebbleloggitch we made our way by a long canal-like stillwater through a land wherein no man—not even an Indian, perhaps—has ever made his home, for it lies through a weird, lonely marsh—a sort of meadow which no reaper ever harvested, where none but the wild moose ever feeds.

We were nearing the edge of the unknown now. One of the guides, Del, I think, had been through this stillwater once before, a long time ago. At the end of it, he knew, lay the upper Shelburne River, which was said to flow through a sheet of water called Irving Lake. But where the river entered the lake and where it left it was for us to learn. Already forty miles or more from our starting point, straight into the wilderness, we were isolated from all mankind, and the undiscovered lay directly before. At the end of the stillwater Del said:

"Well, gentlemen, from this on you know as much of the country as I do. All I know is what I've heard, and that's not much. I guess most of it we'll have to learn for ourselves."

Chapter Eleven

By lonely tarn, mid thicket deep,

The she-moose comes to bear

Her sturdy young, and she doth keep

It safely guarded there.

We got any amount of fly-casting in the Pebbleloggitch stillwater, but no trout. I kept Del dodging and twice I succeeded in hooking him, though not in a vital spot. I could have done it, however, if he had sat still and given me a fair chance. I could land Del even with the treetop cast, but the trout refused to be allured. As a rule, trout would not care to live in a place like that. There would not be enough excitement and activity. A trout prefers a place where the water is busy—where the very effort of keeping from being smashed and battered against the rocks insures a good circulation and a constitution like a steel spring. I have taken trout out of water that would have pulverized a golf ball in five minutes. The fiercer the current—the greater the tumult—the more cruel and savage the rocks, the better place it is for trout.

Neither do I remember that we took anything in the Shelburne above Irving Lake, for it was a good deal like the stillwater, with only a gentle riffle here and there. Besides, the day had become chill, and a mist had fallen upon this lonely world—a wet white, drifting mist that was closely akin to rain. On such a day one does not expect trout to rise, and is seldom disappointed. Here and there, where the current was slow-moving and unruffled, Eddie, perhaps, would have tried his dry flies, but never a trout was seen to break water, and it is one of the tenets of dry-fly fishing that a cast may only be made where a trout has been seen to rise—even then, only after a good deal of careful maneuvering on shore to reach the proper spot on the bank without breaking the news to the trout. It wasn't a pleasant time to go wriggling through marsh grass and things along the shore, so it is just as well that there was no excuse for doing it.

As it was, we paddled rather silently down the still river, considerably impressed with the thought that we were entering a land to us unknown—that for far and far in every direction, beyond the white mist that shut us in and half-obliterated the world, it was likely that there was no human soul that was not of our party and we were quieted by the silence and the loneliness on every hand.

Where the river entered the lake there was no dashing, tumbling water. In fact, we did not realize that we had reached the lake level until the shores on either hand receded, slowly at first, and then broadly widening, melted away and were half lost in the mist.

The feeling grew upon me, all at once, that we were very high here. There were no hills or ridges that we could see, and the outlines of such timber as grew along the shore seemed low. It was as if we had reached the top of the world, where there were no more hills—where the trees had been obliged to struggle up to our altitude, barely to fringe us round. As for course now, we had none. Our map was of the vaguest sort. Where the outlet was we could only surmise.

In a general way it was supposed to be at the "other end" of the lake, where there was said to be an old dam, built when the region was lumbered, long ago. But as to the shape of the lake, and just where that "other end" might lie, when every side except the bit of shore nearest at hand was lost in the wet, chill mist, were matters for conjecture and experiment. We paddled a little distance and some islands came out of the gray veil ahead—green Nova Scotia islands, with their ledges of rock, some underbrush and a few sentinel pines. We ran in close to these, our guides looking for moose or signs of them.

I may say here that no expedition in Nova Scotia is a success without having seen at least one moose. Of course, in the hunting season, the moose is the prime object, but such is the passion for this animal among Nova Scotia guides, that whatever the season or the purpose of the expedition, and however triumphant its result, it is accounted a disappointment and a failure by the natives when it ends without at least a glimpse of a moose.

We were in wonderful moose country now; the uninvaded wild, where in trackless bog and swamp, or on the lonely and forgotten islands the she-moose secludes herself to bear and rear her young. That Charlie and Del were more absorbed in the possibility of getting a sight of these great, timid, vanishing visions of animal life—and perhaps a longer view of a little black, bleating calf—than in any exploration for the other end of the Shelburne River was evident. They clung and hovered about those islands, poking the canoes into every nook and corner, speaking in whispers, and sitting up straight at sight of any dark-looking stump or bunch of leaves. Eddie, too, seemed a good deal interested in the moose idea. I discovered presently that he was ambitious to send a specimen of a moose calf, dead or alive, to the British Museum, and would improve any opportunity to acquire that asset.

I may say that I was opposed to any such purpose. I am overfond of Eddie, and I wanted him to have a good standing with the museum people, but I did not like the idea of slaughtering a little calf moose before its mother's very eyes, and I did not approve of its capture, either. Even if the mother moose could be convinced that our intentions were good, and was willing to have her offspring civilized and in the British Museum, or Zoo, or some other distinguished place, I still opposed the general scheme. It did not seem to me that a calf moose tied either outside or inside of our tent for a period of weeks, to bleat and tear around, and to kick over and muss up things generally, would be a proper feature to add to a well-ordered camp, especially if it kept on raining and we had to bring him inside. I knew that eventually he would own that tent, and probably demand a sleeping bag. I knew that I should have to give him mine, or at least share it with him.

I stated and emphasized these views and insisted that we go over toward the half-obscured shore, where there appeared to be an opening which might be the river. We did go over there, at length, and there was, in fact, an opening, but it was made by a brook entering the lake instead of leaving it. Our memorandum of information declared that a stream called the Susketch emptied into the lake somewhere, and we decided to identify this as the place. We went up a little way to a good looking pool, but there were no trout—at least, they refused to rise, though probably the oldest and mossiest inhabitant of that place had never had such an opportunity before. Back to the lake again, we were pretty soon hovering about the enchanted islands, which seemed to rise on every hand.

It was just the sort of a day to see moose, Del said, and there was no other matter that would stand in importance against a proposition like that. I became interested myself, presently, and dropped my voice to a whisper and sat up at every black spot among the leaves. We had just about given it up at length, when all at once Del gave the canoe a great shove inshore, at the same time calling softly to the other canoe, which had already sheared off into the lake.

They were with us in an instant and we were clambering out. I hadn't seen a thing, but Del swore that he had caught a glimpse of something black that moved and disappeared.

Of course we were clad in our wet-weather armor. I had on my oilskins, and what was more, those high, heavy wading boots that came up under my arms. It is no easy matter to get over even level ground rapidly with a rig like that, and when it comes to scaling an island, full of ledges and holes and underbrush and vines, the problem becomes complex. Del and Charlie, with their shoepacks, distanced me as easily as if I had been sitting still, while that grasshopper, Eddie, with only the lightest sort of waders, skipped and scampered away and left me plunging and floundering about in the brush, with scarcely the possibility of seeing anything, even if it were directly in front of my nose.

As a matter of fact, I didn't care anything about seeing moose, and was only running and making a donkey of myself because the others were doing it, and I had caught a touch of their disease.

Suddenly, I heard Charlie call, "There they are! There they go!" and with a wild redoubled effort I went headlong into a deep pit, half-filled with leaves and brush, and muck of various sorts. This, of course, would seem to assassinate any hope I might have of seeing the moose, but just then, by some occult process, Charles, the Strong, discovered my disaster, and with that prowess which has made him famous yanked me out of the mess, stood me on my feet and had me running again, wallowing through the bushes toward the other side of the little island whence the moose had fled.

"There they go—they are swimming!" I heard Del call, and then Eddie:

"I see em! I see em!" and then Charles's voice, a little ahead of me:

"Hurry! Hurry! They've got over to the shore!"

I reached the shore myself just then—our shore, I mean— on all fours and full of scratches and bruises, but not too late, for beyond a wide neck of water, on the mainland, two dark phantoms drifted a little way through the mist and vanished into the dark foliage behind.

It was only a glimpse I had and I was battered up and still disordered, more or less, with the ivy poison. But somehow I was satisfied. For one thing, I had become infected with a tinge of the native enthusiasm about seeing the great game of the woods, and then down in my soul I rejoiced that Eddie had failed to capture the little calf. Furthermore, it was comforting to reflect that even from the guides' point of view, our expedition, whatever else might come, must be considered a success.

We now got down to business. It was well along toward evening, and though these days were long days, this one, with its somber skies and heavy mist, would close in early. We felt that it was desirable to find the lake's outlet before pitching our tents, for the islands make rather poor camping places and lake fishing is apt to be slow work. We wanted to get settled in camp on the lower Shelburne before night and be ready for the next day's sport.

We therefore separated, agreeing upon a signal of two shots from whichever of us had the skill or fortune to discover the outlet. The other canoe faded into the mist below the islands while we paddled slowly toward the gray green shores opposite. When presently we were all alone, I was filled, somehow, with the feeling that must have come over those old Canadian voyageurs who were first to make their way through the northlands, threading the network of unknown waters. I could not get rid of the idea that we were pioneers in this desolate spot, and so far as sportsmen were concerned, it may be that we were.

Chapter Twelve

The lake is dull with the drifting mist,

And the shores are dim and blind;

And where is the way ahead, to-day,

And what of the path behind?

Along the wet, blurred shore we cruised, the mist getting thicker and more like rain. Here and there we entered some little bay or nook that from a distance looked as if it might be an outlet. Eventually we lost all direction and simply investigated at random wherever any appearance seemed inviting. Once we went up a long slough and were almost ready to fire the signal shots when we discovered our mistake. It seemed a narrow escape from the humiliation of giving a false alarm. What had become of the others we did not know. Evidently the lake was a big one and they might be miles away. Eddie had the only compass, though this would seem to be of no special advantage.

At last, just before us, the shore parted—a definite, wide parting it was, that when we pushed into it did not close and come to nothing, but kept on and on, opening out ahead. We went a good way in, to make sure. The water seemed very still, but then we remembered the flatness of the country. Undoubtedly this was the outlet, and we had discovered it. It was only natural that we should feel a certain elation in our having had the good fortune—the instinct, as it were—to proceed aright. I lifted my gun and it was with a sort of triumphant flourish that I fired the two signal shots.

It may be that the reader will not fully understand the importance of finding a little thing like the outlet of a lake on a wet, disagreeable day when the other fellows are looking for it, too; and here, to-day, far away from that northern desolation, it does not seem even to me a very great affair whether our canoe or Eddie's made the discovery. But for some reason it counted a lot then, and I suppose Del and I were unduly elated over our success. It was just as well that we were, for our period of joy was brief. In the very instant while my finger was still touching the trigger, we heard come soggily through the mist, from far down the chill, gray water, one shot and then another.

I looked at Del and he at me.

"They've found something, too," I said. "Do you suppose there are two outlets? Anyhow, here goes," and I fired again our two shots of discovery, and a little later two more so that there might be no mistake in our manifest. I was not content, you see, with the possibility of being considered just an ordinary ass, I must establish proof beyond question of a supreme idiocy in the matter of woodcraft. That is my way in many things. I know, for I have done it often. I shall keep on doing it, I suppose, until the moment when I am permitted to say, "I die innocent."

"They only think they have found something," I said to Del now. "It's probably the long slough we found a while ago. They'll be up here quick enough," and I fired yet two more shots, to rub it in.

But now two more shots came also from Eddie, and again
two more. By this time we had pushed several hundred
yards farther into the opening, and there was no doubt but
that it was a genuine river. I was growing every moment
more elated with our triumph over the others and in
thinking how we would ride them down when they finally
had to abandon their lead and follow ours, when all at once
Del, who had been looking over the side of the canoe grew
grave and stopped paddling.

"There seems to be a little current here," he pointing down
to the grass which showed plainly now in the clear water,
"yes—there—is—a current," he went on very slowly, his
voice becoming more dismal at every word, "but it's going
the wrong way!"

I looked down intently. Sure enough, the grass on the
bottom pointed back toward the lake.

"Then it isn't the Shelburne, after all," I said, "but another
river we've discovered."

Del looked at me pathetically.

"It's the Shelburne, all right," he nodded, and there was
deep suffering in his tones, "oh, yes, it's the Shelburne—
only it happens to be the upper end—the place where we
came in. That rock is where you stopped to make a few
casts."

No canoe ever got out of the upper Shelburne River quicker
than ours. Those first old voyageurs of that waste region
never made better time down Irving Lake. Only, now and
then, I fired some more to announce our coming, and to
prepare for the lie we meant to establish that we only had

been replying to their shots all along and not announcing anything new and important of our own.

But it was no use. We had guilt written on our features, and we never had been taught to lie convincingly. In fact it was wasted effort from the start. The other canoe had been near enough when we entered the trap to see us go in, and even then had located the true opening, which was no great distance away. They jeered us to silence and they rode us down. They carefully drew our attention to the old log dam in proof that this was the real outlet; they pointed to the rapid outpouring current for it was a swift boiling stream here—and asked us if we could tell which way it was flowing. For a time our disgrace was both active and complete. Then came a diversion. Real rain—the usual night downpour—set in, and there was a scramble to get the tents up and our goods under cover.

Yet the abuse had told on me. One of my eyes—the last to yield to the whisky treatment, began to throb a good deal—and I dragged off my wet clothes, got on a dry garment (the only thing I had left by this time that was dry) and worked my way laboriously, section by section, into my sleeping bag, after which Eddie was sorry for me—as I knew he would be—and brought me a cup of tea and some toast and put a nice piece of chocolate into my mouth and sang me a song. It had been a pretty strenuous day, and I had been bruised and cold and wet and scratched and humiliated. But the tea and toast put me in a forgiving spirit, and the chocolate was good, and Eddie can sing. I was dry, too, and reasonably warm. And the rain hissing into the campfire at the door had a soothing sound.

Chapter Thirteen

Now take the advice that I do not need—

That I do not heed, alway:

For there's many a fool can make a rule

Which only the wise obey.

As usual, the clouds had emptied themselves by morning. The sky was still dull and threatening, and from the tent door the water of the lake was gray. But the mist had gone, and the islands came out green and beautiful. The conditions made it possible to get some clothing decently smoked and scorched, which is the nearest approach to dryness one is ever likely to achieve in the woods in a rainy season.

I may say here that the time will come—and all too soon, in a period of rain—when you will reach your last dry suit of underwear—and get it wet. Then have a care. Be content to stay in a safe, dry spot, if you can find one—you will have to go to bed, of course, to do it until something is dry—that is, pretty dry. To change from one wet suit to another only a little less so is conducive neither to comfort nor to a peaceful old age. Above all, do not put on your night garment, or garments, for underwear, for they will get wet, too; then your condition will be desperate.

I submit the above as good advice. I know it is good advice for I did not follow it. I have never followed good advice— I have only given it. At the end of several nights of rain and moist days, I had nothing really dry but my nightshirt and one slipper and I think Eddie's condition was not so far removed. What we did was to pick out the least damp of our things and smoke and scorch them on a pole over the campfire until they had a sort of a half-done look, like bread toasted over a gas jet; then suddenly we would seize them and put them on hot and go around steaming, and smelling of leaf smoke and burnt dry goods—these odors blended with the fragrance of camphor, tar and pennyroyal, with which we were presently saturated in every pore. For though it was said to be too late for black flies and too early for mosquitoes, the rear guard of the one and the advance guard of the other combined to furnish us with a good deal of special occupation. The most devoted follower of the Prophet never anointed himself oftener than we did, and of course this continuous oily application made it impossible to wash very perfectly; besides, it seemed a waste to wash off the precious protection when to do so meant only another immediate and more thorough treatment.

I will dwell for a moment on this matter of washing. Fishing and camping, though fairly clean recreations, will be found not altogether free from soiling and grimy tendencies, and when one does not or cannot thoroughly remove the evidences several times a day, they begin to tell on his general appearance. Gradually our hands lost everything original except their shape. Then I found that to shave took off a good deal of valuable ointment each time, and I approved of Eddie's ideas in this direction to the extent of following his example. I believe, though, that I washed myself longer than he did—that is, at stated intervals. Of course we never gave up the habit altogether. It would break out sporadically and at unexpected moments, but I do not recall that these lapses ever became dangerous or offensive. My recollection is that Eddie gave up washing as a mania, that morning at the foot of Irving Lake and that I held out until the next sunrise. Or it may have been only until that evening—it does not matter. Washing is a good deal a question of pride, anyway, and pride did not count any more. Even self-respect had lost its charm.

In the matter of clothing, however, I wish to record that I never did put on my nightdress for an undergarment. I was tempted to do so, daily, but down within me a still small voice urged the rashness of such a deed and each night I was thankful for that caution. If one's things are well smoked and scorched and scalded and put on hot in the morning, he can forget presently that they are not also dry, and there is a chance that they may become so before night; but to face the prospect of getting into a wet garment to sleep, that would have a tendency to destroy the rare charm and flavor of camp life. In time I clung to my dry nightshirt as to a life-belt. I wrapped it up mornings as a jewel, buried it deep in the bottom of my bag, and I locked the bag. Not that Eddie did not have one of his own—it may be that he had a variety of such things—and as for the guides, I have a notion that they prefer wet clothes. But though this was a wild country, where it was unlikely that we should meet any living soul, there was always the possibility of a stray prospector or a hunter, and a dry garment in a wet time is a temptation which should not be put in any man's way. Neither that nor the liquor supply. When we left our camp—as we did, often—our guns, our tackle, even our purses and watches, were likely to be scattered about in plain view; but we never failed to hide the whisky. Whisky is fair loot, and the woodsman who would scorn to steal even a dry shirt would carry off whisky and revel in his shame.

There were quantities of trout in the lower Shelburne, and in a pool just below the camp, next morning, Eddie and I took a dozen or more—enough for breakfast and to spare—in a very few minutes. They were lively fish—rather light in color, but beautifully marked and small enough to be sweet and tender, that is, not much over a half-pound weight. In fact, by this time we were beginning to have a weakness for the smaller fish. The pound-and-upward trout, the most plentiful size, thus far, were likely to be rather dry and none too tender. When we needed a food supply, the under-sized fish were more welcome, and when, as happened only too rarely, we took one of the old-fashioned New England speckled beauty dimensions—that is to say, a trout of from seven to nine inches long and of a few ounces weight—it was welcomed with real joy. Big fish are a satisfaction at the end of a line and in the landing net, but when one really enters upon a trout diet—when at last it becomes necessary to serve them in six or seven different ways to make them go down—the demand for the smallest fish obtainable is pretty certain to develop, while the big ones are promptly returned with good wishes and God-speed to their native element.

For of course no true sportsman ever keeps any trout he cannot use. Only the "fish-hog" does that. A trout caught on a fly is seldom injured, and if returned immediately to the water will dart away, all the happier, it may be, for his recent tug-of-war. He suffers little or no pain in the tough cartilages about his mouth and gills (a fact I have demonstrated by hooking the same fish twice, both marks plainly showing on him when taken) and the new kind of exercise and experience he gets at the end of the line, and his momentary association with human beings, constitute for him a valuable asset, perhaps to be retailed in the form of reminiscence throughout old age. But to fling him into a canoe, to gasp and die and be thrown away, that is a different matter. That is a crime worse than stealing a man's lunch or his last dry undershirt, or even his whisky.

In the first place, kill your trout the moment you take him out of the water—that is, if you mean to eat him. If he is too big, or if you already have enough, put him back with all expedition and let him swim away. Even if he does warn the other trout and spoil the fishing in that pool, there are more pools, and then it is likely you have fished enough in that one, anyway. Come back next year and have another battle with him. He will be bigger and know better what to do then. Perhaps it will be his turn to win.

In the matter of killing a fish there are several ways to do it. Some might prefer to set him up on the bank and shoot at him. Another way would be to brain him with an ax. The guides have a way of breaking a trout's neck by a skillful movement which I never could duplicate. My own method is to sever the vertebræ just back of the ears—gills, I mean—with the point of a sharp knife. It is quick and effective.

I don't know why I am running on with digression and advice this way. Perhaps because about this period I had had enough experience to feel capable of giving advice. A little experience breeds a lot of advice. I knew a man once—— [3]

Chapter Fourteen

Oh, never a voice to answer here,

And never a face to see—

Mid chill and damp we build our camp

Under the hemlock tree.

In spite of the rains the waters of the Shelburne were too low at this point to descend in the canoes. The pools were pretty small affairs and the rapids long, shallow and very ragged. It is good sport to run rapids in a canoe when there is plenty of swift water and a fair percentage of danger. But these were dangerous only to the canoes, which in many places would not even float, loaded as we were. It became evident that the guides would have to wade and drag, with here and there a carry, to get the boats down to deeper water—provided always there was deeper water, which we did not doubt.

Eddie and I set out ahead, and having had our morning's fishing, kept pretty well to the bank where the walking was fairly good. We felt pleasant and comfortable and paid not much attention to the stream, except where a tempting pool invited a cast or two, usually with prompt returns, though we kept only a few, smaller fish.

We found the banks more attractive. Men had seldom disturbed the life there, and birds sang an arm's length away, or regarded us quietly, without distrust. Here and there a hermit thrush—the sweetest and shyest of birds— himself unseen, charmed us with his mellow syllables. Somehow, in the far, unfretted removal of it all, we felt at peace with every living thing, and when a partridge suddenly dropped down on a limb not three yards away, neither of us offered to shoot, though we had our rifles and Eddie his B. M. license to kill and skin and hence to eat, and though fish were at a discount and game not overplentiful.

And then we were rewarded by a curious and beautiful exhibition. For the partridge was a mother bird, and just at our feet there was a peeping and a scampering of little brown balls that disappeared like magic among the leaves—her fussy, furry brood.

I don't think she mistrusted our intent—at least, not much. But she wanted to make sure. She was not fully satisfied to have us remain just there, with her babies hiding not two yards away. She dropped on the ground herself, directly in front of us—so close that one might almost touch her—and letting one of her wings fall loosely, looked back at us over her shoulder as if to say, "You see, it is broken. If you wish, you can catch me, easily."

So we let her fool us—at least, we let her believe we were deceived—and made as if to stoop for her, and followed each time when she ran a few steps farther ahead, until little by little she had led us away from her family. Then when she was sure that we really did not want her or her chickens, but cared only to be amused, she ran quickly a little way farther and disappeared, and we saw her no more.

Within a minute or two from that time she was probably
back with her little folks, and they were debating as to
whether we were bird or beast, and why we carried that
curious combination of smells.

It was such incidents as this that led us on. The morning
was gone, presently, and we had no means of knowing how
far we had come. It seemed to us but a short way. We
forgot the windings of the stream, some of which we had
eluded by cut-offs, and how many hard places there would
be for Del and Charlie to get over with the canoes. As a
matter of fact we rather expected them to overtake us at any
time, and as the pools became deeper and longer and the
rapids somewhat more navigable we feared to leave the
stream on the chance of being passed. It was about one
o'clock when we reached a really beautiful stretch of water,
wide and deep, and navigable for an indefinite distance.
Here we stopped to get fish for luncheon, and to wait for
the boats, which we anticipated at any moment.

It was a wonderful place to fish. One could wade out and
get long casts up and down, and the trout rose to almost any
fly. Eddie caught a white perch at last and I two yellow
ones, not very plentiful in these waters and most desirable
from the food point of view. The place seemed really
inexhaustible. I think there were few trout larger than
fourteen inches in length, but of these there were a great
many, and a good supply of the speckled beauty size. When
we had enough of these for any possible luncheon demand,
and were fairly weary of casting and reeling in, we
suddenly realized that we were hungry; also that it was well
into the afternoon and that there were no canoes in sight.
Furthermore, in the enthusiasm of the sport we had both of
us more than once stepped beyond the gunwales of our
waders and had our boots full of water, besides being

otherwise wet. Once, in fact, I had slipped off a log on all fours, in a rather deep place. It began to be necessary that we should have a camp and be fed. Still we waited hopefully, expecting every moment to see the canoes push around the bend.

Eventually we were seized with misgivings. Could the guides have met with shipwreck in some desperate place and disabled one or both of the canoes, perhaps losing our stores? The thought was depressing. Was it possible that they had really passed us during some period when we had left the water, and were now far ahead? We could not believe it. Could it be that the river had divided at some unseen point and that we had followed one fork and they another? It did not seem probable. Perhaps, after all, we had come farther than we believed, and they had been delayed by the difficulties of navigation.

But when another hour passed and they did not appear or answer to our calls, the reason for their delay did not matter. We were wet, cold and hungry. Food and fire were the necessary articles. We had not a scrap of food except our uncooked fish, and it would be no easy matter, without ax or hatchet, to get a fire started in those rain-soaked woods. Also, we had no salt, but that was secondary.

Eddie said he would try to build a fire if I would clean some fish, but this proved pretty lonesome work for both of us. We decided to both build and then both clean the fish. We dug down under the leaves for dry twigs, but they were not plentiful. Then we split open some dead spruce branches and got a few resinous slivers from the heart of them, a good many in fact, and we patiently gathered bits of reasonably dry bark and branches from under the sheltered side of logs and rocks and leaning trees.

We meant to construct our fire very carefully and we did. We scooped a little hollow in the ground for draught, and laid in some of the drier pieces of bark, upon which to pile our spruce slivers. Upon these in turn we laid very carefully what seemed to be our driest selections of twigs, increasing the size with each layer, until we laid on limbs of goodly bulk and had a very respectable looking heap of fuel, ready for lighting on the windward side.

Our mistake was that we did not light it sooner. The weight of our larger fuel had pressed hard upon our little heap of spruce slivers and flattened it, when it should have remained loose and quickly inflammable, with the larger fuel lying handy, to be added at the proper moment. As it was, the tiny blaze had a habit of going out just about the time when it ought to have been starting some bigger material. When we did get a sickly flame going up through the little damp mess of stuff, there was a good deal more smoke than fire and we were able to keep the blaze alive only by energetic encouragement in the form of blowing.

First Eddie would get down on his hands, with his chin against the ground and blow until he was apoplectic and blind with smoke, and then I would take my turn. I never saw two full-grown men so anxious over a little measly fire in my life. We almost forgot that we were perishing with cold and hunger ourselves in our anxiety to keep the spark of life in that fire.

We saved the puny thing, finally, and it waxed strong. Then we put in a good deal of time feeding and nursing our charge and making it warm and comfortable before we considered ourselves. And how did the ungrateful thing repay us? By filling our eyes with smoke and chasing us from side to side, pursuing us even behind trees to blind and torture us with its acrid smarting vapors. In fact, the perversity of campfire smoke remains one of the unexplained mysteries. I have seen a fire properly built between two tents—with good draught and the whole wide sky to hold the smoke—suddenly send a column of suffocating vapor directly into the door of the tent, where there was no draught, no room, no demand at all for smoke. I have had it track me into the remotest corner of my sleeping-bag and have found it waiting for me when I came up for a breath of air. I have had it come clear around the tent to strangle me when I had taken refuge on the back side. I have had it follow me through the bushes, up a tree, over a cliff——

As I was saying, we got the fire going. After that the rest was easy. It was simply a matter of cleaning a few trout, sticking them on sticks and fighting the smoke fiend with one hand while we burnt and blackened the trout a little with the other, and ate them, sans salt, sans fork, sans knife, sans everything. Not that they were not good. I have never eaten any better raw, unsalted trout anywhere, not even at Delmonico's.

The matter of getting dry and warm was different. It is not the pleasantest thing in the world, even by a very respectable fire such as we had now achieved, to take off all of one's things without the protection of a tent, especially when the woods are damp and trickly and there is a still small breath of chill wind blowing, and to have to hop and skip, on one foot and then on the other, to keep the circulation going while your things are on a limb in the smoke, getting scalded and fumigated, and black edged here and there where the flame has singed up high. It's all in a day's camping, of course, and altogether worth while, but when the shades of night are closing in and one is still doing a spectral dance about a dying fire, in a wet wood, on a stomach full of raw trout, then the camping day seems pretty long and there is pressing need of other diversion.

It was well toward night when we decided that our clothes were scorched enough for comfortable wear, and a late hour it was, for the June days in the north woods are long. We had at no time lost sight of the river, and we began to realize the positive necessity of locating our guides and canoes. We had given up trying to understand the delay. We decided to follow back up the river until we found them, or until we reached some other branch which they might have chosen. It was just as we were about to begin this discouraging undertaking that far up the bend we heard a call, then another. We answered, both together, and in the reply we recognized the tones of Charles the Strong.

Presently they came in sight—each dragging a canoe over the last riffle just above the long hole. A moment later we had hurried back to meet two of the weariest, wettest, most bedraggled mortals that ever poled and dragged and carried canoe. All day they had been pulling and lifting; loading, unloading and carrying those canoes and bags and baskets over the Shelburne riffles, where not even the lightest craft could float. How long had been the distance they did not know, but the miles had been sore, tedious miles, and they had eaten nothing more than a biscuit, expecting at every bend to find us waiting.

It was proper that we should make camp now at the first inviting place. We offered to stop right there, where our fire was already going, but it was decided that the ground was a poor selection, being rather low. We piled into the canoes and shot down the long hole, while the light of evening was fading from the sky. Several hundred yards below, the water widened and the bank sloped higher. It seemed an attractive spot and we already knew the fishing in these waters. But as a final test Eddie made a cast as we rounded, tossing his flies into an inviting swirl just below a huge bowlder. For some reason we had put on three flies, and when he finally got his mess of fish into the net, there were three trout—all good ones—one on each fly.

We decided to camp there, for good luck, and to stay until we were fully repaired for travel. No camp was ever more warmly welcomed, or ever will be more fondly remembered by us all.

Chapter Fifteen

To-night, to-night, the frost is white,

Under the silver moon;

And lo, I lie, as the hours go by,

Freezing to death in June.

The reader will have gathered by this time that I had set out
with only a hazy idea of what camping in Nova Scotia
would be like. I think I had some notion that our beds
would be down in the mud as often as not, and sticky and
disagreeable—something to be endured for the sake of the
day's sport. Things were not as I expected, of course.
Things never are. Our beds were not in the mud—not
often—and there were days—chill, wet, disheartening
days—when I looked forward to them and to the campfire
blaze at the tent door with that comfort which a child finds
in the prospect of its mother's arm.

On the whole, I am sure our camps were more commodious
than I had expected them to be; and they were pretentious
affairs, considering that we were likely to occupy them no
more than one night. We had three tents—Eddie's, already
described; a tent for the guides, of about the same
proportions, and a top or roof tent, under which we dined
when it rained. Then there was a little porch arrangement
which we sometimes put out over the front, but we found it

had the bad habit of inviting the smoke to investigate and permeate our quarters, so we dedicated the little porch fly to other uses. A waterproof ground cloth was spread between our stretcher beds, and upon the latter, as mentioned before, were our sleeping-bags; also our various bundles, cozily and conveniently bestowed. It was an inviting interior, on the whole something to anticipate, as I have said.

Yet our beds were not perfect. Few things are. I am a rather large man, and about three o'clock in the morning I was likely to wake up somewhat cramped and pinched together from being so long in the little canvas trough, with no good way of putting out my arms; besides being a little cold, maybe, because about that hour the temperature seemed to make a specialty of dropping low enough to get underneath one's couch and creep up around the back and shoulders. It is true it was June, but June nights in Nova Scotia have a way of forgetting that it is drowsy, scented summertime; and I recall now times when I looked out through the tent flap and saw the white frost gleaming on the trees, and wondered if there was any sum of money too big to exchange for a dozen blankets or so, and if, on the whole, perishing as I was, I would not be justified in drugging Eddie in taking possession of his sleeping-bag. He had already given me one of the woolen pockets, for compared with mine his was a genuine Arctic affair, and, I really believe, kept him disgustingly warm, even when I was freezing. I was grateful, of course, for I should have perished early in the fight without it. I was also appreciative. I knew just how much warmer a few more of those soft, fleecy pockets would make me, especially on those nights when I woke about the cheerless hour of three, to find the world all hard and white, with the frost fingers creeping down my shoulder blades and along my spine.

Then it was I would work around and around—slowly and with due deliberation of movement, for a sleeping-bag is not a thing of sudden and careless revolution—trying to find some position or angle wherein the cold would not so easily and surely find my vitals. At such a time, the desire for real comfort and warmth is acute, and having already one of Eddie's pockets and realizing its sterling worth— also that no more than two feet away from me he lay warm and snug, buried in the undue luxury of still other pockets—I may confess now I was goaded almost to the point of arising and taking peremptory possession of the few paltry pockets that would make my lot less hard.

Sooner or later, I suppose, I should have murdered Eddie for his blankets if he had not been good to me in so many ways. Daily he gave me leaders, lines, new flies and such things; nightly he painted my scratches with new skin. On the slightest provocation he would have rubbed me generously with liniment, for he had a new, unopened bottle which he was dying to try. Then there was scarcely an evening after I was in bed—I was always first to go, for Eddie liked to prepare his bed unhurriedly—that he did not bring me a drink, and comfort me with something nice to eat, and maybe sing a little while he was "tickling" his own bed (there is no other name for it), and when he had finished with the countless little tappings, and pattings, and final touches which insured the reposeful comfort of his couch, he would place the candle lantern just between, where each could see equally well and so read a little in order that we might compose our minds for rest.

Chapter Sixteen

Now snug, the camp—the candle-lamp,

Alighted stands between—

I follow "Alice" in her tramp

And you your "Folly Queen."

In the matter of Eddie's reading, however, I was not wholly satisfied. When we had been leaving the little hotel, he had asked me, suddenly, what I would take for reading in the woods. He added that he always read a little at night, upon retiring, and from his manner of saying it, I assumed that such reading might be of a religious nature.

Now, I had not previously thought of taking anything, but just then I happened to notice lying upon the table a copy of "Alice in Wonderland," evidently belonging to the premises, and I said I would take that. I had not foregathered with Alice and the White Rabbit for a good while, and it seemed to me that in the depths of an enchanted wood I might properly and profitably renew their acquaintance. The story would hardly offend Eddie, even while he was finding solace in his prayer-book.

I was only vaguely troubled when on the first night of our little reading exercise I noticed that Eddie's book was not of the sort which I had been led to expect, but was a rather thick, suspicious-looking affair, paper-bound. Still, I reflected, it might be an ecclesiastical treatise, or even what is known as a theological novel, and being absorbed just then in an endeavor to accompany Alice into the wonderful garden I did not investigate.

What was my surprise—my shock, I may say—next morning, on picking up the volume, to discover that it was printed in a foreign language, and that language French—always a suspicious thing in print—and to learn further, when by dint of recalling old school exercises, I had spelled out the author's name and a sentence here and there, that not only was it in that suspicious language, but that it was a novel, and of a sort—well, of course there is only one thing worse than an English translation of a French novel, and that is a French novel which cannot be translated—by any one in this country, I mean, who hopes to keep out of jail.

I became absorbed in an endeavor to unravel a passage here and there myself. But my French training had not fitted me for the task. My lessons had been all about the silk gloves of my uncle's children or of the fine leather shoes of my mother's aunt, and such innocent things. I could find no reference to them in Eddie's book. In fact I found on almost every page reference to things which had nothing to do with wardrobe of any sort, and there were words of which I had the deepest suspicion. I was tempted to fling the volume from me with a burning blush of shame. Certainly it was necessary to protest against the introduction of the baleful French novel into this sylvan retreat.

I did so, later in the day, but it was no use. Eddie had already gulped down some twenty pages of the poison and would not listen to reason. There was a duchess in the book, and I knew immediately from the lame excuses he made for this person that she was not at all a proper associate for Eddie, especially in this remote place. I pleaded in vain. He had overtaken the duchess on the third page, and the gaud of her beauty was in his eyes. So it came to pass that while I was following gentle little Alice and the White Rabbit through a land of wonder and dreams, Eddie, by the light of the same candle, was chasing this butterfly of folly through a French court at the rate of some twenty finely printed pages every night, translating aloud here and there, until it sometimes became necessary for me to blow out the candle peremptorily, in order that both of us might compose our minds for needed slumber.

Perhaps I am dwelling unnecessarily upon our camp detail, but, after all, the tent, with its daily and nightly round becomes a rather important thing when it is to be a habitation for a period of weeks of sun and storm; and any little gem of experience may not be wholly unwasted.

Then there is the matter of getting along without friction, which seems important. A tent is a small place, and is likely to contain a good many things—especially in bad weather—besides yourselves. If you can manage to have your things so the other fellow will stumble over them as infrequently as possible, it is just as well for him, and safer for you. Also, for the things. Then, too, if you will make your beds at separate times, as we did, one remaining outside, or lying in a horizontal position among his own supplies while the other is in active operation, you are less likely to rub against each other, which sometimes means to rub in the wrong direction, with unhappy results. Of course forbearance is not a bad asset to have along, and a small measure of charity and consideration. It is well to take one's sense of humor, too, and any little remnant of imagination one may have lying about handy at the moment of starting. Many a well-constructed camp has gone to wreck during a spell of bad weather because one or more of its occupants did not bring along imagination and a sense of humor, or failed to produce these articles at the critical moment. Imagination beautifies many a desolate outlook— a laugh helps over many a hard place.

Chapter Seventeen

Oh, the pulses leap where the fall is steep,

And the rocks rise grim and dark,

With the swirl and sweep of the rapids deep,

And the joy of the racing bark.

We established a good camp on the Shelburne and remained in it for several days. For one thing, our canoes needed a general overhauling after that hard day on the rocks. Also, it rained nightly, and now and then took a turn at it during the day, to keep in practice.

We minded the rain, of course, as it kept us forever cooking our clothes, and restrained a good deal of activity about the camp. Still, we argued that it was a good thing, for there was no telling what sort of water lay ahead and a series of rock-strewn rapids with low water might mean trouble.

On the whole, we were willing to stay and put up with a good deal for the sport in that long pool. There may be better fishing on earth than in the Shelburne River between Irving and Sand lakes, but it will take something more than mere fisherman's gossip to convince either Eddie or me of that possibility. We left the guides and went out together one morning, and in less than three hours had taken full fifty fish of a pound each, average weight. We took off our top flies presently and fished with only one, which kept us busy enough, and always one of us had a taut line and a curved rod; often both at one time.

We began to try experiments at last, and I took a good fish on one of the funny little scale-winged flies (I had happily lost the Jock Scott with two hooks early in the campaign) and finally got a big fellow by merely tying a bit of white absorbent cotton to a plain black hook.

Yet curious are the ways of fish. For on the next morning— a perfect trout day, with a light southwest wind and running clouds, after a night of showers—never a rise could we get. We tried all the casts of the day before—the Parmcheenie, the Jenny Lind, the Silver Doctor and the Brown Hackle. It was no use. Perhaps the half a hundred big fellows we had returned to the pool had warned all the others; perhaps there was some other unwritten, occult law which prohibited trout from feasting on this particular day. Finally Eddie, by some chance, put on a sort of a Brown Hackle affair with a red piece of wool for a tail—he called it a Red Tag fly, I think—and straightway from out of the tarry black depths there rose such a trout as neither of us had seen the day before.

After that, there was nothing the matter with Eddie's fishing. What there was about this brown, red-tailed joke that tickled the fancy of those great silly trout, who would have nothing to do with any other lure, is not for me to say. The creature certainly looked like nothing that ever lived, or that they could ever have imagined before. It seemed to me a particularly idiotic combination and I could feel my respect for the intelligence of trout waning. Eddie agreed with me as to that. He said he had merely bought the thing because it happened to be the only fly he didn't have in his collection and there had been a vacant place in his fly-book. He said it was funny the trout should go for it as they did, and he laughed a good deal about it. I suppose it was funny, but I did not find it very amusing. And how those crazy-headed trout did act. In vain I picked out flies with the red and brown colors and tossed them as carefully as I could in just the same spots where Eddie was getting those great whoppers at every cast. Some mysterious order from the high priest of all trout had gone forth that morning, prohibiting every sort and combination of trout food except this absurd creature of which the oldest and mossiest trout had never dreamed. That was why they went for it. It was the only thing not down on the list of proscribed items.

There was nothing for me to do at last but to paddle Eddie around and watch him do some of the most beautiful fishing I have ever seen, and to net his trout for him, and take off the fish, and attend to any other little wants incident to a fisherman's busy day. I did it with as good grace as I could, of course, and said I enjoyed it, and tried not to be nasty and disagreeable in my attitude toward the trout, the water, Eddie, and the camp and country in general. But, after all, it is a severe test, on a day like that, to cast and cast and change flies until you have wet every one in your book, without even a rise, and to see the other chap taking great big black and mottled fellows—to see his rod curved like a whip and to watch the long, lithe body leaping and gleaming in the net.

But the final test, the climax, was to come at evening. For when the fish would no longer rise, even to the Red Tag, we pulled up to the camp, where Eddie of course reported to the guides his triumph and my discomfiture. Then, just as he was opening his fly-book to put the precious red-tailed mockery away, he suddenly stopped and stared at me, hesitated, and held up another—that is, two of them, side by side.

"So help me!" he swore, "I didn't know I had it! I must have forgotten I had one, and bought another, at another time. Now, I had forgotten that, too. So help me!"

If I hadn't known Eddie so well—his proclivity for buying, and forgetting, and buying over again—also his sterling honor and general moral purity—the fishes would have got him then, Red Tag and all. As it was, I condescended to accept the second fly. I agreed that it was not such a bad production, after all, though I altered my opinion again, next morning, for whatever had been the embargo laid on other varieties of trout bait the day before, it was on now, and there was a general rising to anything we offered— Doctors, Parmcheenie, Absorbent Cotton—any old thing that skimmed the water and looked big and succulent.

We broke camp that morning and dropped down toward the next lake—Sand Lake, it would be, by our crude map and hazy directions. There are no better rapids and there is no more lively fishing than we had on that run. There was enough water for us to remain in the canoes, and it was for the most part whirling, swirling, dashing, leaping water— shooting between great bowlders—plunging among cruel-looking black rocks—foaming into whirlpools below, that looked ready to swamp our light craft, with stores, crew, tackle, everything.

It was my first exhibition of our guides' skill in handling their canoes. How they managed to just evade a sharp point of rock on one side and by a quick twist escape shipwreck from a bowlder or mass of bowlders on the other, I fail to comprehend. Then there were narrow boiling channels, so full of obstructions that I did not believe a chip could go through with entire safety. Yet somehow Del the Stout and Charles the Strong seemed to know, though they had never traveled this water before, just where the water would let the boats pass, just where the stones were wide enough to let us through—touching on both sides, sometimes, and ominously scraping on the bottom, but sliding and teetering into the cauldron below, where somehow we did not perish, perhaps because we shot so quickly through the foam. In the beginning I remembered a few brief and appropriate prayers, from a childhood where such things were a staff of comfort, and so made my peace with the world each time before we took the desperate plunge. But as nothing seemed to happen—nothing fatal, I mean—I presently gave myself up to the pure enjoyment of the tumult and exhilaration, without disturbing myself as to dangers here or hereafter.

I do not believe the times that the guides got out of the canoes to ease them over hard places would exceed twice, and not oftener than that were we called on to assist them with the paddles. Even when we wished to do so, we were often requested to go on fishing, for the reason, I suppose, that in such a place one's unskilled efforts are likely to be misdirected with fatal results. Somewhat later we were to have an example of this kind—but I anticipate.

We went on fishing. I never saw so many fish. We could take them as we shot a rapid, we could scoop them in as we leaped a fall. They seemed to be under every stone and lying in wait. There were great black fellows in every maelstrom; there were groups holding receptions for us in the stillwater pools below. It is likely that that bit of the Shelburne River had not been fished before within the memory of any trout then living, and when those red and

blue and yellow flies came tumbling at them, they must
have thought it was great day in the morning and that the
white-faced prophets of big feeding had come. For years,
the trout we returned to those pools will tell their friends
and descendants of the marvels and enchantments of that
day.

I had given up my noibwood as being too strenuous in its
demands for constant fishing, but I laid aside the light
bamboo here in this high-pressure current and with this
high-speed fishing, where trout sometimes leaped clear of
the water for the fly cast on the foam far ahead, to be
swinging a moment later at the end of the line almost as far
behind. No very delicate rod would improve under a strain
like that, and the tough old noibwood held true, and nobody
cared—at least I didn't—whether the tip stayed set or not. It
was bent double most of the time, anyway, and the rest of
the time didn't matter.

I don't know how many fish I took that day, but Eddie kept
count of his, and recorded a total of seventy-four between
camp and the great, splendid pool where the Shelburne
foams out into Sand Lake, four miles or such a matter,
below.

I do know that we lost two landing nets in that swift water,
one apiece, and this was a serious matter, for there were but
two more, both Eddie's, and landing nets in the wilderness
are not easy to replace. Of fish we kept possibly a dozen,
the smallest ones. The others—larger and wiser now—are
still frolicking in the waters of the Shelburne, unless some
fish-hog has found his way to that fine water, which I think
doubtful, for a fish-hog is usually too lazy and too stingy to
spend the effort and time and money necessary to get there.

Chapter Eighteen

There's nothing that's worse for sport, I guess,

Than killing to throw away;

And there's nothing that's better for recklessness

Than having a price to pay.

We had other camp diversions besides reading. We had shooting matches, almost daily, one canoe against the other, usually at any stop we happened to make, whether for luncheon or to repair the canoes, or merely to prospect the country. On rainy days, and sometimes in the evening, we played a game of cards known under various names—I believe we called it pedro. At all events, you bid, and buy, and get set back, and have less when you get through than you had before you began. Anyhow, that is what my canoe did on sundry occasions. I am still convinced that Del and I played better cards than the other canoe, though the score would seem to show a different result. We were brilliant and speculative in our playing. They were plodders and not really in our class. Genius and dash are wasted on such persons.

I am equally certain that our shooting was much worse than theirs, though the percentage of misses seemed to remain in their favor. In the matter of bull's-eyes—whenever such accidents came along—they happened to the other canoe, but perhaps this excited our opponents, for there followed periods of wildness when, if their shots struck anywhere, it was impossible to identify the places. At such periods Eddie was likely to claim that the cartridges were blanks, and perhaps they were. As for Del and me, our luck never varied like that. It remained about equally bad from day to day—just bad enough to beat the spectacular fortunes of Eddie and Charles the Strong.

In the matter of wing-shooting, however—that is to say, shooting when we were on the wing and any legitimate quarry came in view—my recollection is that we ranked about alike. Neither of us by any chance ever hit anything at all, and I have an impression that our misses were about equally wide. Eddie may make a different claim. He may claim that he fired oftener and with less visible result than I. Possibly he did fire oftener, for he had a repeating rifle and I only a single shot, but so far as the result is concerned, if he states that his bullets flew wider of the mark, such a claim is the result of pure envy, perhaps malice. Why, I recall one instance of a muskrat whose skin Eddie was particularly desirous of sending to those museum folks in London—all properly mounted, with their names (Eddie's and the muskrat's) on a neat silver plate, so that it could stand there and do honor to us for a long time—until the moths had eaten up everything but the plate, perhaps, and Eddie struck the water within two or three feet of it (the muskrat, of course) as much as a dozen times, while such shots as I let go didn't hit anything but the woods or the sky and are, I suppose, still buried somewhere in the quiet bosom of nature. I am glad to unload that sentence. It was getting top-heavy, with a muskrat and moths and a silver plate in it. I could shoot some holes in it with a little practice, but inasmuch as we didn't get the muskrat, I will let it stand as a stuffed specimen.

I am also glad about the muskrat. Had he perished, our pledge would have compelled us to eat him, and although one of Eddie's text-books told a good deal about their food value and seven different ways of cooking them, I was averse to experimenting even with one way. I have never really cared for muskrats since as a lad I caught twenty of them one night in a trammel net. Up to that hour the odor of musk had never been especially offensive to me, but twenty muskrats in a net can compound a good deal of perfumery. We had to bury the net, and even then I never cared much about it afterwards. The sight of it stirred my imagination, and I was glad when it was ripped away from us by a swift current one dark night, it being unlawful to set a trammel net in that river, and therefore sinful, by daylight.

It was on Sand Lake that Eddie gave the first positive demonstration of his skill as a marksman. Here, he actually made a killing. True, it was not a wing shot, but it was a performance worthy of record. A chill wet wind blew in upon us as we left the river, and a mist such as we had experienced on Irving Lake, with occasional drifts of rain, shut us in. At first it was hard to be certain that we were really on a lake, for the sheet of water was long and narrow, and it might be only a widening of the river. But presently we came to an island, and this we accepted as identification. It was the customary island, larger than some, but with the bushes below, the sentinel pines, and here and there a gaunt old snag—bleached and dead and lifting its arms to the sky. On one of these dead ones we made out, through the mist, a strange dark bunch about the size of a barn door and of rather irregular formation.

Gradually nearing, we discovered the bunch to be owls—great horned owls—a family of them, grouped on the old tree's limbs in solid formation, oblivious to the rain, to the world, to any thought of approaching danger.

Now, the great horned owl is legitimate quarry. The case against him is that he is a bird of prey—a destroyer of smaller birds and an enemy of hen roosts. Of course if one wanted to go deeply into the ethics of the matter, one might say that the smaller birds and the chickens are destroyers, too, of bugs and grasshoppers and things, and that a life is a life, whether it be a bird or a bumble-bee, or even a fish-worm. But it's hard to get to the end of such speculations as that. Besides, the owl was present, and we wanted his skin. Eddie crept close in with his canoe, and drew a careful bead on the center of the barn door. There was an angry little spit of powder in the wet, a wavering movement of the dark, mist-draped bunch, a slow heaving of ghostly pinions and four silent, feathered phantoms drifted away into the white gloom. But there was one that did not follow. In vain the dark wings heaved and fell. Then there came a tottering movement, a leap forward, and half-fluttering, half-plunging, the heavy body came swishing to the ground.

Yet unused to the battle as he was, for he was of the younger brood, he died game. When we reached him he was sitting upright, glaring out of his great yellow eyes, his talons poised for defense. Even with Eddie's bottle of new skin in reserve, it was not considered safe to approach too near. We photographed him as best we could, and then a shot at close range closed his brief career.

I examined the owl with considerable interest. In the first place I had never seen one of this noble species before, and this was a beautiful specimen. Also, his flesh, being that of a young bird, did not appeal to warrant the expression tough as a boiled owl, which the others remembered almost in a chorus when I referred to our agreement concerning the food test of such game as we brought down. I don't think any of us wanted to eat that owl. I know I didn't, but I had weakened once—on the porcupine, it may be remembered—and the death of that porcupine rested heavily upon me, especially when I remembered how he had whined and grieved in the moment of dying. I think I had a notion that eating the owl would in some measure atone for the porcupine. I said, with such firmness as I could command, and all day I repeated at intervals, that we would eat the owl.

We camped rather early that afternoon, for it was not pleasant traveling in the chill mist, and the prospect of the campfire and a snug tent was an ever-present temptation. I had suggested, also, that we ought to go ashore in time to cook the owl for supper. It might take time to cook him.

We did not especially need the owl. We had saved a number of choice small trout and we were still able to swallow them when prepared in a really palatable form. Eddie, it is true, had condemned trout at breakfast, and declared he would have no more of them, but this may have been because there were flapjacks. He showed no disposition to condemn them now. When I mentioned the nice, tender owl meat which we were to have, he really looked longingly at the trout and spoke of them as juicy little fellows, such as he had always liked. I agreed that they would be good for the first course, and that a bird for supper would make out a sumptuous meal. I have never known Eddie to be so kind to me as he was about this time. He offered me some leaders and flies and even presented me with a silver-mounted briar-root pipe, brought all the way from London. I took the things, but I did not soften my heart. I was born in New England and have a conscience. I cannot be bribed like that.

I told the guides that it would be better to begin supper right away, in order that we might not get too hungry before the owl was done. I thought them slow in their preparations for the meal. It was curious, too, for I had promised them they should have a piece of the bird. Del was generous. He said he would give his to Charles. That he never really cared much for birds, anyhow. Why, once, he said, he shot a partridge and gave it away, and he was hungry, too. He gave it to a boy that happened along just then, and when another partridge flew up he didn't even offer to shoot it. We didn't take much stock in that story until it dawned upon us that he had shot the bird out of season, and the boy had happened along just in time to be incriminated by accepting it as a present. It was better to have him as a partner than a witness.

As for Charles, he affected to be really eager for owl meat. He said that all his life he had looked forward to this time. Still, he was slow, I thought. He seemed about as eager for supper as a boy is to carry in the evening wood. He said that one of the canoes leaked a little and ought to be pitched right away. I said it was altogether too damp for such work and that the canoe would wait till morning. Then he wanted to look up a spring, though there were two or three in plain sight, within twenty yards of the camp. I suspected at last that he was not really anxious to cook the owl and was trying to postpone the matter until it was too late for him (the owl) to get properly done before bedtime. Then I became firm. I said that a forest agreement was sacred. That we were pledged to the owl before we shot him, and that we would keep our promise to the dead, even to the picking of his bones.

Wood was gathered then, and the fire blazed. The owl's breast—fat and fine it looked—was in the broiler, and on the fire. There it cooked—and cooked. Then it cooked some more and sent up an appetizing smell. Now and then, I said I thought the time for it had come, but there was a burden of opinion that more cooking would benefit the owl. Meantime, we had eaten a pan or two of trout and a few other things—the bird of course being later in the bill of fare. At most dinners I have attended, this course is contemplated with joy. It did not seem to be on this occasion. Eddie agreed with Del that he had never cared much for bird, anyway, and urged me to take his share. I refused to deprive him of it. Then he said he didn't feel well, and thought he really ought not to eat anything more. I said grimly that possibly this was true, but that he would eat the owl.

It was served then, fairly divided and distributed, as food is when men are on short rations. I took the first taste—I was always venturesome—a little one. Then, immediately, I wished I had accepted Eddie's piece. But meantime he had tasted, too—a miserly taste—and then I couldn't have got the rest of it for money.

For there was never anything so good as that breast of young owl. It was tender, it was juicy, it was as delicately flavored as a partridge, almost. Certainly it was a dainty morsel to us who had of late dealt so largely in fish diet. Had we known where the rest of that brood of owls had flown to we should have started after them, then and there.

Extract from my diary that night: "Eddie has been taken with a slight cramp, and it has occurred to him that the owl meat, though appetizing, may be poisonous. He is searching his medicine bag for remedies. His disaster is merely punishment for the quantity of other food he ate beforehand, in his futile effort to escape the owl."

Chapter Nineteen

Then scan your map, and search your plans,

And ponder the hunter's guess—

While the silver track of the brook leads back

Into the wilderness.

We looked for moose again on Sand Lake, but found only signs. On the whole, I thought this more satisfactory. One does not have to go galloping up and down among the bushes and rocks to get a glimpse of signs, but may examine them leisurely and discuss the number, character and probable age of these records, preserving meanwhile a measure of repose, not to say dignity.

Below Sand Lake a brook was said to enter. Descending from the upper interior country, it would lead us back into regions more remote than any heretofore traveled. So far as I could learn, neither of our guides had ever met any one who even claimed in know this region, always excepting the imaginative Indian previously mentioned. Somewhere in these uncharted wilds this Indian person had taken trout "the size of one's leg."

Regardless of the dimensions of this story, it had a fascination for us. We wished to see those trout, even if they had been overrated. We had been hurrying, at least in spirit, to reach the little water gateway that opened to a deeper unknown where lay a chain of lakes, vaguely set down on our map as the Tobeatic [4] waters. At some time in the past the region had been lumbered, but most of the men who cut the timber were probably dead now, leaving only a little drift of hearsay testimony behind.

It was not easy to find the entrance to the hidden land. The foliage was heavy and close along the swampy shore, and from such an ambush a still small current might flow unnoticed, especially in the mist that hung about us. More than once we were deceived by some fancied ripple or the configuration of the shore. Del at length announced that just ahead was a growth of a kind of maple likely to indicate a brook entrance. The shore really divided there and a sandy waterway led back somewhere into a mystery of vines and trees.

We halted near the mouth of the little stream for lunch and consultation. It was not a desirable place to camp. The ground was low and oozy and full of large-leaved greenhousy-looking plants. The recent rains had not improved the character of the place. There was poison ivy there, too, and a delegation of mosquitoes. We might just as well have gone up the brook a hundred yards or so, to higher and healthier ground, but this would not have been in accord with Eddie's ideas of exploration. Explorers, he said, always stopped at the mouth of rivers to debate, and to consult maps and feed themselves in preparation for unknown hardships to come. So we stopped and sat around in the mud, and looked at some marks on a paper—made by the imaginative Indian, I think—and speculated as to whether it would be possible to push and drag the canoes up the brook, or whether everything would have to go overland.

Personally, the prospect of either did not fill me with enthusiasm. The size of the brook did not promise much in the way of important waters above or fish even the size of one's arm. However, Tobeatic exploration was down on the cards. Our trip thus far had furnished only a hint of such mystery and sport as was supposed to lie concealed somewhere beyond the green, from which only this little brooklet crept out to whisper the secret. Besides, I had learned to keep still when Eddie had set his heart on a thing. I left the others poring over the hieroglyphic map, and waded out into the clean water of the brook. As I looked back at Del and Charlie, squatting there amid the rank weeds, under the dark, dripping boughs, with Eddie looking over their shoulders and pointing at the crumpled paper, spread before them, they formed a picturesque group—such a one as Livingstone or Stanley and their followers might have made in the African jungles. When I told Eddie of this he grew visibly prouder and gave me two new leaders and some special tobacco.

We proceeded up the stream, Eddie and I ahead, the guides pushing the loaded canoes behind. It was the brook of our forefathers—such a stream as might flow through the valley meadows of New England, with trout of about the New England size, and plentiful. Lively fellows, from seven to nine inches in length, rose two and three at almost every cast. We put on small flies and light leaders and forgot there were such things as big trout in Nova Scotia. It was joyous, old-fashioned fishing—a real treat for a change.

We had not much idea how far we were to climb this water stairway, and as the climb became steeper, and the water more swift, the guides pushed and puffed and we gave them a lift over the hard places—that is, Eddie did. I was too tired to do anything but fish.

As a rule, the water was shallow, but there were deep holes. I found one of them presently, by mistake. It was my habit to find holes that way—places deeper than my waders, though the latter came to my shoulders. It seemed necessary that several times daily I should get my boots full of water. When I couldn't do it in any other way I would fall over something and let the river run into them for a while. I called to Eddie from where I was wallowing around, trying to get up, with my usual ballast.

"Don't get in here!" I said.

He was helping the boys over a hard place just then, tugging and sweating, but he paused long enough to be rude and discourteous.

"I don't have to catch my trout in my boots," he jeered, and the guides were disrespectful enough to laugh. I decided that I would never try to do any of them a good turn again. Then suddenly everything was forgotten, for a gate of light opened out ahead, and presently we pushed through and had reached the shores of as lovely a sheet of water as lies in the great north woods. It was Tupper Lake, by our calculation, and it was on the opposite side that Tobeatic Brook was said to enter. There, if anywhere, we might expect to find the traditional trout. So far as we knew, no one had looked on these waters since the old lumbering days. Except for exploration there was no reason why any one should come. Of fish and game there were plenty in localities more accessible. To me, I believe the greatest joy there, as everywhere in the wilderness—and it was a joy that did not grow old—was the feeling that we were in a region so far removed from clanging bells and grinding wheels and all the useful, ugly attributes of mankind.

We put out across the lake. The land rose rather sharply beyond, and from among the trees there tumbled out a white foaming torrent that made a wide swirling green pool where it entered. We swept in below this aquarium, Eddie taking one side and I the other. We had on our big flies now and our heavy leaders. They were necessary. Scarcely had a cast gone sailing out over the twisting water when a big black and gold shape leaped into the air and Eddie had his work cut out for him. A moment later my own reel was singing, and I knew by the power and savage rushes that I had something unusual at the other end.

"Trout as big as your leg!" we called across to each other, and if they were not really as big as that, they were, at all events, bigger than anything so far taken—as big as one's arm perhaps—one's forearm, at least, from the hollow of the elbow to the fingertips. You see how impossible it is to tell the truth about a trout the first time. I never knew a fisherman who could do it. There is something about a fish that does not affiliate with fact. Even at the market I have known a fish to weigh more than he did when I got him home. We considered the imaginative Indian justified, and blessed him accordingly.

Chapter Twenty

You may slip away from a faithful friend

And thrive for an hour or two,

But you'd better be fair, and you'd better be square,

Or something will happen to you.

We took seventeen of those big fellows before we landed, enough in all conscience. A point just back of the water looked inviting as a place to pitch the tents, and we decided to land, for we were tired. Yet curious are the ways of fishermen: having had already too much, one becomes greedy for still more. There was an old dam just above, unused for a generation perhaps, and a long, rotting sluiceway through which poured a torrent of water. It seemed just the place for the king of trouts, and I made up my mind to try it now before Eddie had a chance. You shall see how I was punished.

I crept away when his back was turned, taking his best and longest-handled landing net (it may be remembered I had lost mine), for it would be a deep dip down into the sluice. The logs around the premises were old and crumbly and I had to pick my way with care to reach a spot from which it would be safe to handle a big trout. I knew he was there. I never had a stronger conviction in my life. The projecting ends of some logs which I chose for a seat seemed fairly permanent and I made my preparations with care. I put on a new leader and two large new flies. Then I rested the net in a handy place, took a look behind me and sent the cast down the greased lightning current that was tearing through the sluice.

I expected results, but nothing quite so sudden. Neither did I know that whales ever came so far up into fresh-water streams. I know it was a whale, for nothing smaller could have given a yank like that; besides, in the glimpse I had of him he looked exactly like pictures I have seen of the leviathan who went into commission for three days to furnish passage for Jonah and get his name in print. I found myself suddenly grabbing at things to hold on to, among them being Eddie's long-handled net, which was of no value as ballast, but which once in my hand I could not seem to put down again, being confused and toppling.

As a matter of fact there was nothing satisfactory to get hold of in that spot. I had not considered the necessity of firm anchorage when I selected the place, but with a three-ton trout at the end of a long line, in a current going a thousand miles a minute, I realized that it would be well to be lashed to something permanent. As it was, with my legs swinging over that black mill-race, my left hand holding the rod, and my right clutching the landing net, I was in no position to withstand the onset of a battle such as properly belongs to the North Pacific Ocean where they have boats and harpoons and long coiled lines suitable to such work.

Still, I might have survived—I might have avoided complete disaster, I think—if the ends of those two logs I selected as a seat had been as sound as they looked. Of course they were not. They were never intended to stand any such motions as I was making. In the brief moment allowed me for thought I realized this, but it was no matter. My conclusions were not valuable. I remember seeing the sluice, black, and swift, suddenly rise to meet me, and of dropping Eddie's net as I went down. Then I have a vision of myself shooting down that race in a wild toboggan ride, and a dim, splashy picture of being pitched out on a heap of brush and stones and logs below.

When I got some of the water out of my brains so I could think with them, I realized, first, that I was alive, still clutching my rod and that it was unbroken. Next, that the whale and Eddie's landing net were gone. I did not care so especially much about the whale. He had annoyed me. I was willing to part with him. Eddie's net was a different matter. I never could go back without that. After all his goodness to me I had deceived him, slipped away from him, taken his prized net—and lost it. I had read of such things; the Sunday-school books used to be full of similar incidents. And even if Eddie forgave me, as the good boy in the books always did, my punishment was none the less sure. My fishing was ended. There was just one net left. Whatever else I had done, or might do, I would never deprive Eddie of his last net. I debated whether I should go to him, throw myself on his mercy—ask his forgiveness and offer to become his special guide and servant for the remainder of the trip—or commit suicide.

But presently I decided to make one try, at least, to find the net. It had not been thrown out on the drift with me, for it was not there. Being heavy, it had most likely been carried along the bottom and was at present lodged in some deep crevice. It was useless, of course; still, I would try.

I was not much afraid of the sluice, now that I had been introduced to it. I put my rod in a place of safety and made my way to the upper end of the great trough. Then I let myself down carefully into the racing water, bracing myself against the sides and feeling along the bottom with my feet. It was uncertain going, for the heavy current tried hard to pull me down. But I had not gone three steps till I felt something. I could not believe it was the net. I carefully steadied myself and—down, down to my elbow. Then I could have whooped for joy, for it was the net. It had caught on an old nail or splinter, or something, and held fast.

Eddie was not at the camp, and the guides were busy getting wood. I was glad, for I was wet and bruised and generally disturbed. When I had changed my things and recovered a good deal, I sat in the shade and smoked and arranged my fly-book and other paraphernalia, and brooded on the frailty of human nature and the general perversity and cussedness of things at large. I had a confession all prepared for Eddie, long before he arrived. It was a good confession—sufficiently humble and truthful without being dangerous. I had tested it carefully and I did not believe it could result in any disagreeable penance or disgrace on my part. It takes skill to construct a confession like that. But it was wasted. When Eddie came in, at last, he wore a humble hang-dog look of his own, and I did not see the immediate need of any confession.

"I didn't really intend to run off from you," he began sheepishly. "I only wanted to see what was above the dam, and I tried one or two of the places up there, and they were all so bully I couldn't get away. Get your rod, I want to take you up there before it gets too late."

So the rascal had taken advantage of my brief absence and slipped off from me. In his guilty haste he had grabbed the first landing net he had seen, never suspecting that I was using the other. Clearly I was the injured person. I regarded him with thoughtful reproach while he begged me to get my rod and come. He would take nothing, he said, but a net, and would guide for me. I did not care to fish any more that day; but I knew Eddie—I knew how his conscience galled him for his sin and would never give him peace until he had made restitution in full. I decided to be generous.

We made our way above the dam, around an old half-drained pond, and through a killing thicket of vines and brush to a hidden pool, faced with slabs and bowlders. There, in that silent dim place I had the most beautiful hour's fishing I have ever known. The trout were big, gamy fellows and Eddie was alert, obedient and respectful. It was not until dusk that he had paid his debt to the last fish—had banished the final twinge of remorse.

Our day, however, was not quite ended. We must return to camp. The thicket had been hard to conquer by daylight. Now it was an impenetrable wall of night and thorns. Across the brook looked more open and we decided to go over, but when we got there it proved a trackless, swampy place, dark and full of pitfalls and vines. Eddie, being small and woods-broken could work his way through pretty well, but after a few discouragements I decided to wade down the brook and through the shallow pond above the dam. At least it could not be so deadly dark there.

It was heart-breaking business. I went slopping and plunging among stumps and stones and holes. I mistook logs for shadows and shadows for logs with pathetic results. The pond that had seemed small and shallow by daylight was big enough and deep enough now. A good deal of the way I went on my hands and knees, but not from choice. A nearby owl hooted at me. Bats darted back and forth close to my face. If I had not been a moral coward I should have called for help. Eddie had already reached camp when I arrived and had so far recovered his spiritual status that he jeered at my condition. I resolved then not to mention the sluice and the landing net at all—ever. I needed an immediate change of garments, of course—the third since morning. [5] It had been a hard, eventful day. Such days make camping remembered—and worth while.

Chapter Twenty-one

Oh, it's well to live high as you can, my boy,

Wherever you happen to roam,

But it's better to have enough bacon and beans

To take the poor wanderers home.

By this time we had reached trout diet per se. I don't know
what per se means, but I have often seen it used and it
seems to fit this case. Of course we were not entirely out of
other things. We had flour for flapjacks, some cornmeal for
mush and Johnnie-cake, and enough bacon to impart flavor
to the fish. Also, we were not wholly without beans—long
may they wave—the woods without them would be a
wilderness indeed. But in the matter of meat diet it was
trout per se, as I have said, unless that means we did not
always have them; in which case I will discard those words.
We did. We had fried trout, broiled trout, boiled trout,
baked trout, trout on a stick and trout chowder. We may
have had them other ways—I don't remember. I know I
began to imagine that I was sprouting fins and gills, and
daily I felt for the new bumps on my head which I was
certain must result from this continuous absorption of brain
food. There were several new bumps, but when I called
Eddie's attention to them, he said they were merely the
result of butting my head so frequently against logs and

stumps and other portions of the scenery. Then he treated them with liniment and new skin.

Speaking of food, I believe I have not mentioned the beefsteak which we brought with us into the woods. It was Eddie's idea, and he was its self-appointed guardian and protector. That was proper, only I think he protected it too long. It was a nice sirloin when we started—thick and juicy and of a deep rich tone. Eddie said a little age would improve it, and I suppose he was right—he most always is. He said we would appreciate it more, too, a little later, which seemed a sound doctrine.

Yet, somehow, that steak was an irritation. It is no easy matter to adjust the proper age of a steak to the precise moment of keen and general appreciation. We discussed the matter a good deal, and each time the steak was produced as a sort of Exhibit A, and on each occasion Eddie decided that the time was not ripe—that another day would add to its food value. I may say that I had no special appetite for steak, not yet, but I did not want to see it carried off by wild beasts, or offered at last on a falling market.

Besides, the thing was an annoyance as baggage. I don't know where we carried it at first, but I began to come upon it in unexpected places. If I picked up a yielding looking package, expecting to find a dry undergarment, or some other nice surprise, it turned out to be that steak. If I reached down into one of the pack baskets for a piece of Eddie's chocolate, or some of his tobacco—for anything, in fact—I would usually get hold of a curious feeling substance and bring up that steak. I began to recognize its texture at last, and to avoid it. Eventually I banished it from the baskets altogether. Then Eddie took to hanging it on a limb near the camp, and if a shower came up suddenly he couldn't rest—he must make a wild rush and take in that steak. I refused at last to let him bring it into the tent, or to let him hang it on a nearby limb. But this made trouble, for when he hung it farther away he sometimes forgot it, and twice we had to paddle back a mile or so to get that steak. Also, sometimes, it got wet, which was not good for its flavor, he said; certainly not for its appearance.

In fact, age told on that steak. It no longer had the deep rich glow of youth. It had a weather-beaten, discouraged look, and I wondered how Eddie could contemplate it in that fond way. It seemed to me that if the time wasn't ripe the steak was, and that something ought to be done about a thing like that. My suggestions did not please Eddie.

I do not remember now just when we did at last cook that steak. I prefer to forget it. Neither do I know what Eddie did with his piece. I buried mine.

Eddie redeemed himself later—that is to say, he produced something I could eat. He got up early for the purpose. When I awoke, a savory smell was coming in the tent. Eddie was squatted by the fire, stirring something in a long-handled frying pan. Neither he nor the guides were communicative as to its nature, but it was good, and I hoped we would have it often. Then they told me what it was. It was a preparation with cream (condensed) of the despised canned salmon which I had denounced earlier in the trip as an insult to live, speckled trout. You see how one's point of view may alter. I said I was sorry now we hadn't brought some dried herring. The others thought it a joke, but I was perfectly serious.

In fact, provisioning for a camping trip is a serious matter. Where a canoe must carry a man and guide, with traps and paraphernalia, and provisions for a three-weeks' trip, the problem of condensation in the matter of space and weight, with amplitude in the matter of quantity, affords study for a careful mind. We started out with a lot of can and bottle goods, which means a good deal of water and glass and tin, all of which are heavy and take up room. I don't think ours was the best way. The things were good—too good to last—but dried fruits—apricots, prunes and the like—would have been nearly as good, and less burdensome. Indeed by the end of the second week I would have given five cents apiece for a few dried prunes, while even dried apples, which I had learned to hate in childhood, proved a gaudy luxury. Canned beans, too, I consider a mistake. You can't take enough of them in that form. No two canoes can safely carry enough canned beans to last two fishermen and two Nova Scotia guides for three weeks. As for jam and the like, why it would take one canoe to carry enough marmalade to supply Del the Stout alone. If there is any such thing as a marmalade cure, I hope Del will take it before I am ready to go into the woods again. Otherwise I shall tow an extra canoe or a marmalade factory.

As I have said, dried things are better; fruits, beans, rice, beef, bacon—maple sugar (for sirup), cornmeal and prepared flour. If you want to start with a few extras in the way of canned stuff, do it, but be sure you have plenty of the staples mentioned. You will have enough water and tin and glass to carry with your condensed milk, your vinegar, a few pickles, and such other bottle refreshments as your tastes and morals will permit. Take all the variety you can in the way of dried staples—be sure they are staples—but cut close on your bulky tinned supplies. It is better to be sure of enough Johnnie-cake and bacon and beans during the last week out than to feast on plum-pudding and California pears the first.

Chapter Twenty-two

Oh, it's up and down the island's reach,

Through thicket and gorge and fen,

With never a rest in their fevered quest,

Hurry the hunter men.

I would gladly have lingered at Tobeatic Dam. It was an ideal place, wholly remote from everything human—a haunt of wonderful trout, peaceable porcupines and tame birds. The birds used to come around the tent to look us over and ask questions, and to tell us a lot about what was going on in the back settlements—those mysterious dim places where bird and beast still dwell together as in the ancient days, their round of affairs and gossip undisturbed. I wanted to rest there, and to heal up a little before resuming the unknown way.

But Eddie was ruthless—there were more worlds to conquer. The spirit of some old ancestor who probably set out to discover the Northwest Passage was upon him. Lower Tobeatic Lake was but a little way above. We pushed through to it without much delay. It was an extensive piece of water, full of islands, lonely rocks and calling gulls, who come to this inland isolation to rear their young.

The morning was clear and breezy and we set on up the lake in the canoes, Eddie, as usual, a good way in advance. He called back to us now and then that this was great moose country, and to keep a sharp lookout as we passed the islands. I did not wish to see moose. The expedition had already acquitted itself in that direction, but Eddie's voice was eager, even authoritative, so we went in close and pointed at signs and whispered in the usual way. I realized that Eddie had not given up the calf moose idea and was still anxious to shine with those British Museum people. It seemed to me that such ambitions were not laudable. I considered them a distinct mar to a character which was otherwise almost perfect. It was at such times that my inclination to drown or poison Eddie was stronger than usual.

He had been behind an island a good while when we thought we heard a shot. Presently we heard it again, and were sure. Del was instantly all ablaze. Two shots had been the signal for moose.

We went around there. I suppose we hurried. I know it was billowy off the point and we shipped water and nearly swamped as we rounded. Behind the island, close in, lay the other canoe, Eddie waving to us excitedly as we came up.

"Two calf meese!" he called (meese being Eddie's plural of moose—everybody knows that mooses is the word). "Little helpless fellows not more than a day or two old. They're too young to swim of course, so they can't get on the island. We've got em, sure!"

"Did you hit either of them?" I asked anxiously.

"No, of course not! I only fired for a signal. They are wholly at our mercy. They were right here just a moment ago. The mother ran, and they hardly knew which way to turn. We can take them alive."

"But, Eddie," I began, "what will you do with them? They'll have to be fed if we keep them, and will probably want to occupy the tents, and we'll have to take them in the canoes when we move."

He was ready for this objection.

"I've been thinking," he said with decision. "Dell and Charlie can take one of the canoes, with the calves in it, and make straight for Milford by the shortest cut. While they're gone we'll be exploring the upper lake."

This was a brief, definite plan, but it did not appeal to me. In the first place, I did not wish to capture those little mooses. Then, too, I foresaw that during the considerable period which must elapse before the guides returned, somebody would have to cook and wash dishes and perform other menial camp labor. I suspected Eddie might get tired of doing guide work as a daily occupation. Also, I was sorry for Charlie and Del. I had a mental picture of them paddling for dear life up the Liverpool River with two calf mooses galloping up and down the canoe, bleating wildly, pausing now and then to lap the faces of the friendly guides and perhaps to bite off an ear or some other handy feature. Even the wild animals would form along the river bank to view a spectacle like that, and I imagined the arrival at the hotel would be something particularly showy. I mentioned these things and I saw that for once the guides were with me. They did not warm to the idea of that trip up the Liverpool and the gaudy homecoming. Eddie was only for a moment checked.

"Well, then," he said, "we'll kill and skin them. We can carry the skins."

This was no better. I did not want those little mooses slaughtered, and said so. But Eddie was roused now, and withered me with judicial severity.

"Look here," he said, and his spectacles glared fiercely. "I'm here as a representative of the British Museum, in the cause of science, not to discuss the protection of dumb creatures. That's another society."

I submitted then, of course. I always do when Eddie asserts his official capacity like that. The authority of the British Museum is not to be lightly tampered with. So far as I knew he could have me jailed for contempt. We shoved our canoes in shore and disembarked. Eddie turned back.

"We must take something to tie their hind legs," he said, and fished out a strap for that purpose. The hope came to me that perhaps, after all, he might not need the strap, but I was afraid to mention it.

I confess I was unhappy. I imagined a pathetic picture of a little innocent creature turning its pleading eyes up to the captor who with keen sheath-knife would let slip the crimson tide. I had no wish to go racing through the brush after those timid victims.

I did, however. The island was long and narrow. We scattered out across it in a thin line of battle, and starting at one end swept down the length of it with a conquering front. That sounds well, but it fails to express what we did. We did not sweep, and we did not have any front to speak of. The place was a perfect tangle and chaos of logs, bushes, vines, pits, ledges and fallen trees. To beat up that covert was a hot, scratchy, discouraging job, attended with frequent escapes from accident and damage. I was satisfied I had the worst place in the line, for I couldn't keep up with the others, and I tried harder to do that than I did to find the little mooses. I didn't get sight of the others after we started. Neither did I catch a glimpse of those little day-old calves, or of anything else except a snake, which I came upon rather suddenly when I was down on my hands and knees, creeping under a fallen tree. I do not like to come upon snakes in that manner. I do not care to view them even behind glass in a museum. An earthquake might strike that museum and break the glass and it might not be easy to get away. I wish Eddie had been collecting snake skins for his museum. I would have been willing for him to skin that one alive.

I staggered out to the other end of the island, at last, with only a flickering remnant of life left in me. I thought Eddie would be grateful for all my efforts when I was not in full sympathy with the undertaking; but he wasn't. He said that by not keeping up with the line I had let the little mooses slip by, and that we would have to make the drive again. I said he might have my route and I would take another. It was a mistake, though. I couldn't seem to pick a better one. When we had chased up and down that disordered island— that dumping ground of nature—for the third time; when I had fallen over every log and stone, and into every hole on it, and had scraped myself in every brush-heap, and not one of us had caught even an imaginary glimpse of those little, helpless, day-old meese, or mooses, or mice for they were harder to find than mice—we staggered out, limp and sore, silently got into our canoes and drifted away. Nobody spoke for quite a while. Nobody had anything to say. Then Charlie murmured reflectively, as if thinking aloud:

"Little helpless fellows—not more than a day or two old——"

And Del added—also talking to himself:

"Too young to swim, of course—wholly at our mercy." Then, a moment later, "It's a good thing we took that strap to tie their hind legs."

Eddie said nothing at all, and I was afraid to. Still, I was glad that my vision of the little creatures pleading for their lives hadn't been realized, or that other one of Del and Charlie paddling for dear life up the Liverpool, with those little mooses bleating and scampering up and down the canoe.

What really became of those calves remains a mystery. Nature teaches her wild children many useful things. Their first indrawn breath is laden with knowledge. Perhaps those wise little animals laughed at us from some snug hiding. Perhaps they could swim, after all, and followed their mother across the island, and so away. Whatever they did, I am glad, even if the museum people have me arrested for it.

Chapter Twenty-three

When the utmost bound of the trail is found—

The last and loneliest lair—

The hordes of the forest shall gather round

To bid you a welcome there.

I do not know what lies above the Tobeatic lakes, but the strip of country between is the true wilderness. It is a succession of swamps and spruce thickets—ideal country for a moose farm or a mosquito hatchery, or for general exploration, but no sort of a place for a Sunday-school picnic. Neither is it a good place to fish. The little brook between the lakes runs along like a chain pump and contains about as many trout. There are one or two pretty good pools, but the effort to reach them is too costly.

We made camp in as dry a place as we could find, but we couldn't find a place as big as the tent that didn't have a spring or a water hole. In fact, the ground was a mass of roots, great and small, with water everywhere between. A spring actually bubbled up between our beds, and when one went outside at night it was a mercy if he did not go plunging into some sort of a cold, wet surprise, with disastrous and profane results. Being the worst camp and the worst country and the poorest fishing we had found, we remained there two days. But this was as it should be. We were not fishermen now, but explorers; and explorers, Eddie said, always court hardships, and pitch their camps in the midst of dangers.

Immediately after our arrival, Eddie and I took one side of the brook and the guides the other, and we set out to discover things, chiefly the upper lake. Of course we would pick the hardest side. We could be depended on to do that. The brook made a long bend, and the guides, who were on the short side, found fairly easy going. Eddie and I, almost immediately, were floundering in a thick miry swamp, where it was hot and breezeless, and where the midges, mooseflies and mosquitoes gave us a grand welcome. I never saw anybody so glad to be discovered as those mooseflies. They were as excited as if we were long lost relatives who had suddenly turned up with a fortune. They swarmed about us and clung to us and tapped us in any convenient place. I did not blame them, of course. Moose diet, year in and year out, would make them welcome anything by way of a change. And what droves of moose there must be in that swamp to support such a muster of flies! Certainly this was the very heart of the moose domain.

Perhaps the reader who has never seen a moosefly may not appreciate the amplitude and vigor of our welcome. The moosefly is a lusty fellow with mottled wings. I believe he is sometimes called the deerfly, though as the moose is bigger and more savage than the deer, it is my opinion that the moosefly is bigger and more savage than any fly that bites the deer. I don't think the deer could survive him. He is about the size of the green-headed horsefly, but of more athletic build. He describes rapid and eager circles about one's head, whizzing meanwhile in a manner which some may like, but which I could not learn to enjoy. His family is large and he has many friends. He brings them all along to greet you, and they all whiz and describe circles at once, and with every circle or two he makes a dip and swipes up about a gill of your lifeblood and guzzles it down, and goes right on whizzing and circling until he picks out a place for the next dip. Unlike the mosquito, the moosefly does not need to light cautiously and patiently sink a well until he strikes a paying vein. His practice on the moose has fitted him for speedier methods. The bill with which he is accustomed to bore through a tough moosehide in a second or two will penetrate a man in the briefest fraction of the time.

We got out of that swamp with no unnecessary delay and made for a spruce thicket. Ordinarily one does not welcome a spruce thicket, for it resembles a tangle of barbed wires. But it was a boon now. We couldn't scratch all the places at once and the spruce thicket would help. We plunged into it and let it dig, and scrape, and protect us from those whizzing, circling blood-gluttons of the swamp. Yet it was cruel going. I have never seen such murderous brush. I was already decorated with certain areas of "New Skin," but I knew that after this I should need a whole one. Having our rods and guns made it harder. In places we were obliged to lie perfectly flat to worm and wriggle through. And the heat was intense and our thirst a torture. Yet in the end it was worth while and the payment was not long delayed. Just beyond the spruce thicket ran a little spring rivulet, cold as ice. Lying on its ferny margin we drank and drank, and the gods themselves cannot create a more exquisite joy than that. We followed the rivulet to where it fed the brook, a little way below. There we found a good-sized pool, and trout. Also a cool breeze and a huge bowlder—complete luxury. We rested on the big stone—I mean I did—and fished, while Eddie was trying to find the way out. I said I would wait there until a relief party arrived. It was no use. Eddie threatened to leave me at last if I didn't come on, and I had no intention of being left alone in that forgotten place.

We struggled on. Finally near sunset of that long, hard June day, we passed out of the thicket tangle, ascended a slope and found ourselves in an open grove of whispering pines that through all the years had somehow escaped the conflagration and the ax. Tall colonnades they formed—a sort of Grove of Dodona which because of some oracle, perhaps, the gods had spared and the conquering vandals had not swept away. From the top of the knoll we caught a glimpse of water through the trees, and presently stood on the shore of Little Tobeatic Lake.

So it was we reached the end of our quest—the farthest point in the unknown. I hardly know what I had expected: trout of a new species and of gigantic size, perhaps, or a strange race of men. Whatever it was, I believe I felt a bit disappointed.

I believe I did not consider it much of a discovery. It was a good deal like other Nova Scotia lakes, except that it appeared to be in two sections and pretty big for its name. But Eddie was rejoiced over our feat. The mooseflies and spruce thickets and the miry swamps we had passed, for him only added relish to this moment of supreme triumph. Eddie would never be the man to go to the Arctics in an automobile or an airship. That would be too easy. He would insist on more embroideries. He would demand all the combined hardships of the previous expeditions. I am at present planning a trip to the South Pole, but I shall leave Eddie at home. And perhaps I shall also be disappointed when I get to the South Pole and find it only a rock in a snowdrift.

We crossed the brook and returned to camp the short way. We differed a good deal as to the direction, and separated once or twice. We got lost at last, for the way was so short and easy that we were below the camp before we knew it. When at last we heard the guides calling (they had long since returned) we came in, blaming each other for several things and were scarcely on speaking terms for as much as five minutes. It was lucky that Charles found a bottle of Jamaica rum and a little pot of honey just then. A mixture of rum and honey will allay irritation due to moosefly and mosquito bites, and to a variety of other causes if faithfully applied.

The matter of mosquitoes was really serious that night. We kept up several smudge fires and sat among them and smoked ourselves like herring. Even then we were not immune. When it came time for bed we brushed the inside of the tent and set our pipes going. Then Eddie wanted to read, as was his custom. I objected. I said that to light a candle would be to invite all those mosquitoes back. He pleaded, but for once I was firm. He offered me some of his best things, but I refused to sell my blood in that way. Finally he declared he had a spread of mosquito net and would put it over the door and every possible opening if I would let him read. I said he might put up the netting and if I approved the job I would then consider the matter. He got out the net—a nice new piece—and began to put it up.

It was a tedious job, arranging that net and fastening it properly by the flickering firelight so that it covered every crack and crevice. When he pulled it down in one place it left an opening in another and had to be poked and pinned and stuffed in and patted down a great many times. From my place inside the tent I could see his nimble shadow on the canvas like some big insect, bobbing and flitting up and down and from side to side. It reminded me of a persistent moth, dipping and dodging about a screen. I drowsily wondered if he would ever get it fixed, and if he wasn't getting hot and tired, for it was a still, sticky night. Yet I suppose I did not realize how hot and tired one might get on such a night, especially after a hard day. When he ceased his lightsome movements at last and crept as carefully as a worm under the net, I expected him to light the candle lamp and read. He did not do so. He gave one long sighing groan of utter exhaustion, dropped down on his bed without removing his clothes and never stirred again until morning.

The net was a great success. Only two mosquitoes got in and they bit Eddie.

Chapter Twenty-four

Apollo has tuned his lute again,

And the pipes of Pan are near,

For the gods that fled from the groves of men

Gather unheeded here.

It was by no means an unpleasant camp, first and last. It was our "Farthest North" for one thing, our deepest point in the wilderness. It would require as much as three or four days travel, even by the quickest and most direct route to reach any human habitation, and in this thought there was charm. It was a curious place, too, among those roots and springs, and the brook there formed a rare pool for bathing. While the others were still asleep I slipped down there for my morning dip. It was early, but in that latitude and season the sun had already risen and filtered in through the still treetops. Lying back in that natural basin with the cool, fresh water slipping over and about one, and all the world afar off and unreal, was to know the joy of the dim, forgotten days when nymphs and dryads sported in hidden pools or tripped to the pipes of Pan. Hemlock and maple boughs lacing above, with blue sky between—a hermit thrush singing: such a pool Diana might have found, shut away in some remote depths of Arcady. I should not have been much surprised to have heard the bay of her hounds in that still early morning, and to have seen her and her train suddenly appear—pursuing a moose, maybe, or merely coming down for a morning swim. Of course I should have secluded myself had I heard them coming. I am naturally a modest person. Besides, I garner from the pictures that Diana is likely to be dangerous when she is in her moods. Eddie bathed, too, later, but the spell was gone then. Diana was far away, the stillness and sun-glint were no more in the treetops, the hermit thrush was no longer in the neighborhood. Eddie grumbled that the water was chilly and that the stones hurt his feet. An hour, sometimes—a moment, even—makes all the difference between romance and reality. Finally, even the guides bathed! We let off fireworks in celebration!

We carried the canoes to the lake that morning and explored it, but there was not much to see. The lake had no inlet that we could find, and Eddie and I lost a dollar apiece with the guides betting on the shape of it, our idea being based upon the glimpse of the evening before. I don't care much for lakes that change their shape like that, and even Eddie seemed willing to abandon this unprofitable region. I suspected, however, that his willingness to take the back track was mainly due to the hope of getting another try at the little mooses, but I resolved to indulge myself no further in any such pastime.

It was hard to drag Eddie by those islands. He wanted to cruise around every one of them and to go ashore and prospect among the débris. He vowed at last that he would come back with Charles from our next camp and explore on his own account. Then, there being a fine breeze directly behind us, he opened out a big umbrella which he had brought along for just such a time, we hitched our canoe on behind, and with that bellying black sail on the forward bow, went down that long, lovely lake in a luxury of idle bliss.

We camped at our old place by the falls and next morning Eddie did in fact return to have another go at the calves. Del was willing to stay at the camp, and I said I would have a quiet day's fishing nearby. It proved an unusual day's fishing for those waters. White perch are not plentiful there, but for some reason a school of them had collected just by our camp. I discovered them by accident and then gave up everything else to get as many of them as possible, for they were a desirable change from trout, and eagerly welcomed. I fished for them by spells all day. Del and I had them for luncheon and we saved a great pan full to be ready for supper, when the others should return.

It was dusk when the other canoe came in. Our companions were very tired, also wet, for it had been a misty day, with showers. Eddie was a bit cross, too. They had seen some calves, he said, but could not get them. His guide agreed with this statement, but when questioned separately their statements varied somewhat as to the reasons of failure. It did not matter. Eddie was discouraged in the calf moose project, I could see that. Presently I began boasting of the big day's sport I had enjoyed, and then to show off I said, "This is how I did it."

Eddie was washing his hands in my perch pool and I had no idea of getting anything—one is not likely to when he wishes to exhibit himself—but I made a cast with the light tackle with two flies on it and immediately had my hands full. For once, I did actually show off when I undertook to do it. I think the only two big perch in that pool seized those flies, and for the next five or ten minutes they were making my reel sing and giving me such sport as only two big white perch on a light tackle can. I brought them to the net at last and Eddie looked on with hungry, envious eyes.

"You don't mean to say you've been taking those things all day," he said.

"All day, more or less. I merely gave this little exhibition to wind up on."

But of course I had to show him the size of the others, then, and he was appeased to the extent of forgetting most of his troubles in a square meal. That quiet day with the white perch, ending as it did with a grand finale, remains one of my fondest memories.

Chapter Twenty-five

You may pick your place—you may choose your hour—

You may put on your choicest flies;

But never yet was it safe to bet

That a single trout would rise.

Back across Tupper Lake and down Sand Brook to the Shelburne. Eddie left the further wilderness with a sigh, for he felt that his chance of getting a moose calf for those museum people was getting slim. A distance—I have forgotten the number of miles—down the Shelburne would bring us to country known to the guides and not remote enough for moose at this season. As Eddie is no longer in this country, I may confess, now, that I was glad.

It was beautiful going, down Sand Brook. There was plenty of water and the day was perfect. There is nothing lovelier in the world than that little limpid stream with its pebbly riffles and its sunlit pools. Sometimes when I think of it now I am afraid that it is no longer there in that far still Arcady, or that it may vanish through some enchantment before I can ever reach it again. Indeed as I am writing here to-day I am wondering if it is really there—hidden away in that quiet unvisited place, when no one is there to see it, and to hear it sing and whisper—if anything is anywhere,

unless some one is there to see and hear. But these are deep
waters. I am prone to stumble, as we have seen, and
somehow my tallest waders never take me through.

I have already said, and repeated, I think, that there is no
better trout fishing than in the Shelburne. The fish now
were not quite so heavy as they had been higher up, but
they were very many. The last half of the miracle of the
loaves and fishes would not have been necessary here had
the multitudes been given some tackle and a few cans of
bait. When we were a little above Kempton Dam, Del
pointed out the first place familiar to him. The woods were
precisely the same—the waters just as fair and fruitful—the
locality just as wild; but somehow as we rounded that bend
a certain breath of charm vanished. The spell of perfect
isolation was gone. I had the feeling that we had emerged
from the enchanted borders of No Man's Land—that we
were entering a land of real places, with the haunts and
habitations of men.

Kempton Dam itself had been used to catch logs, not so
long ago, and Eddie had visited it on a previous occasion.
He still had a fond memory of a very large trout—opinions
differed a trifle as to its exact size—which he had taken
there in a certain pool of golden water, and it was evident
from his talk that he expected to take that trout again, or
some member of its family, or its ghost, maybe,
immediately upon arrival.

It certainly proved an attractive place, and there were any
number of fish. They were not especially large, however.
Even the golden water was fruitful only as to numbers. We
waded among the rocks or stood on the logs, and cast and
reeled and netted and returned fish to the water until we
were fairly surfeited. By that time the guides had the camp

ready, and as it was still early we gave them the rods and watched the sport.

Now a fly-casting tournament at home is a tame entertainment when one has watched the fishing of Nova Scotia guides. To see a professional send a fly sailing out a hundred feet or so in Madison Square Garden is well enough, and it is a meritorious achievement, no doubt, but there is no return except the record and the applause. To see Del the Stout and Charles the Strong doing the same thing from that old log dam was a poem, a picture, an inspiration. Above and below, the rushing water; overhead, the blue sky; on either side, the green of June—the treetops full of the setting sun. Out over the foaming current, skimming just above the surface, the flies would go sailing, sailing—you thought they would never light. They did not go with a swish and a jump, but seemed noiselessly to drift away, as if the lightly swinging rod had little to do with the matter, as if they were alive, in fact, looking for a place to settle in some cozy nook of water where a trout would be sure to be. And the trout were there. It was not the empty tub-fishing of a sportsman's show. The gleam and splash in the pool that seemed remote—that was perhaps thirty yards away in fact—marked the casting limit, and the sharp curve of the rod, and the play to land were more inspiring than any measure of distance or clapping of hands.

Charles himself became so inspired at length with his handsome fishing that he made a rash statement. He declared that he could take five trout in fifteen minutes. He offered to bet a dollar that he could do it. I rather thought he could myself, for the fish were there, and they were not running over large. Still, it was no easy matter to land them in that swift water, and it would be close work. The show would be worth a dollar, even if I lost. Wherefore, I scoffed at his boast and took the bet.

No stipulations were made as to the size of the trout, nor the manner in which they should be taken, nor as to any special locality. It was evident from our guide's preparation that he had evolved certain ideas of his own in the matter. Previously he had been trying to hook a big fish, but it was pretty evident that he did not want any big fish now. There was a little brook—a run-around, as it were—that left the main water just below the dam and came in again at the big pool several hundred yards below. We had none of us touched this tumbling bit of water. It was his idea that it would be full of little trout. He wanted something he could lift out with no unnecessary delay, for time that is likely to be worth over six cents a minute is too expensive to waste in fancy sportsmanship. He selected a short rod and put on some tiny flies. Then he took his position; we got out our watches and called time.

Now, of course, one of the most uncertain things in life to gamble on is fishing. You may pick your place, your day and your time of day. The combination may seem perfect. Yet the fact remains that you can never count with certainty on the result. One might suppose that our guide had everything in his favor. Up to the very moment of his wager he had been taking trout about as rapidly as he could handle them, and from water that had been fished more or less all the afternoon. He knew the particular fly that had been most attractive on this particular day and he had selected a place hitherto unfished—just the sort of a place where small trout seemed likely to abound. With his skill as an angler it would not have surprised me if he had taken his five trout and had more than half the time to spare.

I think he expected to do that himself. I think he did, for he went at it with that smiling sang froid with which one does a sleight of hand trick after long practice. He did not show any appearance of haste in making his first cast, but let the flies go gently out over a little eddying pool and lightly skim the surface of the water, as if he were merely amusing himself by tantalizing those eager little trout. Yet for some reason nothing happened. Perhaps the little trout were attending a party in the next pool. There came no lively snap at those twitching flies—there was not even a silver break on the surface of the water.

I thought our guide's smile faded the least trifle, and that he let the flies go a bit quicker next time. Then when nothing, absolutely nothing, happened again, his look became one of injured surprise. He abandoned that pool and stepping a rock or two downstream, sent the flies with a sharp little flirt into the next—once—twice—it was strange—it was unaccountable, but nothing—not a single thing happened again. It was the same with the next pool, and the next.

There were no special marks of self-confidence, or anything that even resembled deliberation, after this. It was business, strictly business, with the sole idea of taking five fish out of that run, or getting down to a place where five fish could be had. It was a pretty desperate situation, for it was a steep run and there was no going back. To attempt that would be to waste too much precious time. The thing to do was to fish it straight through, with no unnecessary delay. There was no doubt but that this was our guide's programme. The way he deported himself showed that. Perhaps he was not really in a hurry—I want to be just— but he acted as if he was. I have never seen a straddle-bug, but if I ever meet one I shall recognize him, for I am certain he will look exactly like Charles the Strong going down

Tommy Kempton's Run. He was shod in his shoepacks, and he seemed to me to have one foot always in the air wildly reaching out for the next rock—the pair of flies, meanwhile, describing lightning circles over every pool and riffle, lingering just long enough to prove the futility of the cast, to be lying an instant later in a new spot, several yards below. If ever there is a tournament for swift and accurate fly-casting down a flight of rugged stone stairs I want to enter Charles for first honors against the world. But I would not bet on any fish—I want that stipulated. I would not gamble to that extent. I would not gamble even on one fish after being a witness to our guide's experience.

That was a mad race. The rest of us kept a little to one side, out of his way, and not even Del and Eddie could keep up with him. And with all that wild effort not a fish would rise—nor even break water. It was strange—it was past believing—I suppose it was even funny. It must have been, for I seem to recall that we fairly whooped our joy at his acrobatic eagerness. Why, with such gymnastics, Charles did not break his neck I cannot imagine. With the utmost watchfulness I barely missed breaking mine as much as a dozen times.

The time was more than half-expired when we reached the foot of the run, and still no fish, not even a rise. Yet the game was not over. It was supposable that this might be the place of places for fish. Five fish in five minutes were still possible, if small. The guide leaped and waded to a smooth, commanding stone and cast—once—twice, out over the twisting water. Then, suddenly, almost in front of him, it seemed, a great wave rolled up from the depths—there was a swish and a quick curving of the rod—a monstrous commotion, and a struggle in the water. It was a king of fish, we could all see that, and the rest of us gave a shout of approval.

But if Charles was happy, he did not look it. In fact, I have never seen any one act so unappreciative of a big fish, nor handle it in so unsportsmanlike a manner. If I remember his remark it had damn and hell mixed up in it, and these words were used in close association with that beautiful trout. His actions were even worse. He made no effort to play his catch—to work him gradually to the net, according to the best form. Nothing of the kind. You'd have supposed our guide had never seen a big trout before by the way he got hold of that line and yanked him in, hand over hand, regardless of the danger to line and leader and to those delicate little flies, to say nothing of the possibility of losing a fish so handled. Of course the seconds were flying, and landing a fish of that size is not an especially quick process. A three-pound trout in swift water has a way of staying there, even when taken by the main strength and awkwardness system. When only about a yard of line remained between Charlie and the fish, the latter set up such a commotion, and cut up such a series of antics, that it was impossible for one man to hold him and net him, though the wild effort which our guide made to do so seemed amusing to those who were looking on. In fact, if I had not been weak with laughing I might have gone to his rescue sooner. One may be generous to a defeated opponent, and the time limit was on its last minute now. As it was, I waded over presently and took the net. A moment later we had him—the single return in the allotted time, but by all odds the largest trout thus far of the expedition. You see, as I have said, fish are uncertain things to gamble on. Trying for five small ones our fisherman captured one large fish, which at any other moment of the expedition would have been more welcome. Yet even he was an uncertain quantity, for big, strong and active as he was, he suddenly gave a great leap out of the net and was back in the water again. Still, I let him be counted. That was generous.

You might have supposed after that demonstration, Eddie would have been somewhat reticent about backing his skill as a fisherman. But he wasn't. He had just as much faith in his angling, and in his ability to pick good water as if he hadn't seen his guide go down to ignominy and defeat. He knew a place just above the dam, he said, where he could make that bet good. Would I give him the same terms? I would—the offer was open to all comers. I said it was taking candy from children.

We went up to Eddie's place and got out the watches. Eddie had learned something from his guide's exhibition. He had learned not to prance about over a lot of water, and not to seem to be in a hurry. It was such things that invited mirth. He took his position carefully between two great bowlders and during the next fifteen minutes gave us the most charming exhibition of light and delicate fly-casting I have ever witnessed. It was worth the dollar to watch the way in which he sought to wheedle and coax and fascinate those trout, and to study the deft dispatch and grace with which he landed a fish, once hooked. Still he hadn't learned quite enough. He hadn't learned to take five trout in fifteen minutes in that particular place and on that particular evening. Perhaps it was a little late when he began. Perhaps fifteen minutes is a shorter period than it sometimes seems. Three trout completed his score at the end of the allotted time—all fairly large.

Yet I must not fail to add here that a few days later, in other water, both Eddie and his guide made good their wager. Each took his five trout—small ones—in fifteen minutes, and had time to spare. As I have remarked once or twice already, one of the most uncertain things in life to gamble on is fishing.

Chapter Twenty-six

Oh, the waves they pitch and the waves they toss,

And the waves they frighten me;

And if ever I get my boat across

I'll go no more to sea.

We were met by a surprise at our camp. Two men sat there, real men, the first we had seen since we entered the wilderness. Evidently they were natives by their look— trappers or prospectors of some sort. They turned out to be bear hunters, and they looked rather hungrily at the assortment of fish we had brought in—enough for supper and breakfast. Perhaps they had not been to fish so frequently as to bear. I believe they were without tackle, or maybe their luck had been poor—I do not remember. At all events it developed presently that they needed fish, also that they had a surplus of butter of a more recent period than the little dab we had left. They were willing to dicker—a circumstance that filled us with an enthusiasm which we restrained with difficulty. In fact, Del did not restrain his quite enough. He promptly offered them all the fish we had brought in for their extra pound of butter, when we could just as easily have got it for half the number of fish. Of course the fish did not seem especially valuable to us, and we were willing enough to make a meal without them. Still, one can never tell what will happen, and something like six dollars worth of trout—reckoned by New York prices—seems an unnecessary sum to pay for a pound of butter, even in the Nova Scotia woods, though possibly trout will never be worth quite that much there.

All the same, the price had advanced a good deal by next morning, for the wind had shifted to the northeast and it was bleak and blustery. Everybody knows the old rhyme about the winds and the fish—how, when the winds are north or east, the fish bite least, and how, when the winds are south and west, the fish bite best. There isn't much poetry in the old rhyme, but it's charged with sterling truth. Just why a northerly or easterly wind will take away a fish's appetite, I think has never been explained, or why a southerly and westerly wind will start him out hunting for food. But it's all as true as scripture. I have seen trout stop rising with a shifting of the wind to the eastward as suddenly as if they had been summoned to judgment, and I have seen them begin after a cold spell almost before the wind had time to get settled in its new quarter. Of course it had been Del's idea that we could easily get trout enough for breakfast. That was another mistake—we couldn't. We couldn't take them from the river, and we couldn't take them from our bear hunters, for they had gone. We whipped our lines around in that chill wind, tangled our flies in treetops, endangered our immortal souls, and went back to the tents at last without a single thing but our appetites. Then we took turns abusing Del for his disastrous dicker by which he had paid no less than five dollars and seventy-five cents a pound too much for butter, New York market schedule. Our appetites were not especially for trout—only for hearty food of some kind, and as I have said before, we had reached a place where fish had become our real staple. The conditions were particularly hard on Del

himself, for he is a hearty man, and next to jars of
marmalade, baskets of trout are his favorite forage.

In fact, we rather lost interest in our camp, and disagreeable
as it was, we decided to drop down the river to Lake
Rossignol and cross over to the mouth of the Liverpool. It
was a long six-mile ferriage across Rossignol and we could
devote our waste time to getting over. By the end of the trip
the weather might change.

The Shelburne is rough below Kempton Dam. It goes
tearing and foaming in and out among the black rocks, and
there are places where you have to get out of the canoes
and climb over, and the rocks are slippery and sometimes
there is not much to catch hold of. We shot out into the lake
at last, and I was glad. It was a mistake, however, to be
glad just then. It was too soon. The wind had kicked up a
good deal of water, and though our canoes were lighter
than when we started, I did not consider them suited to
such a sea. They pitched about and leaped up into the air,
one minute with the bow entirely out of water, and the next
with it half-buried in the billow ahead. Every other second
a big wave ran on a level with the gunwale, and crested its
neck and looked over and hissed, and sometimes it spilled
in upon us. It would not take much of that kind of freight to
make a cargo, and anything like an accident in that wide,
gray billowy place was not a nice thing to contemplate. A
loaded canoe would go down like a bullet. No one clad as
we were could swim more than a boat's length in that sea.

As we got farther on shore the waves got worse. If
somebody had just suggested it I should have been willing
to turn around and make back for the Shelburne. Nobody
suggested it, and we went on. It seemed to me those far,
dim shores through the mist, five miles or more away,

would never get any closer. I grew tired, too, and my arms ached, but I could not stop paddling. I was filled with the idea that if I ever stopped that eternal dabbing at the water, my end of the canoe would never ride the next billow. Del reflected aloud, now and then, that we had made a mistake to come out on such a day. When I looked over at the other canoe and saw it on the top of a big wave with both ends sticking out in the air, and then saw it go down in a trough of black, ugly water, I realized that Del was right. I knew our canoe was doing just such dangerous things as that, and I would have given any reasonable sum for an adequate life preserver, or even a handy pine plank—for anything, in fact, that was rather more certain to stay on top of the water than this billow-bobbing, birch-bark peanut shell of a canoe.

I suppose I became unduly happy, therefore, when at last we entered the mouth of the Liverpool. I was so glad that I grew gay, and when we started up the rapids I gave Del a good lift here and there by pushing back against the rocks with my paddle, throwing my whole weight on it sometimes, to send the canoe up in style. It is always unwise for me to have a gay reaction like that, especially on Friday, which is my unlucky day. Something is so liable to happen. We were going up a particularly steep piece of water when I got my paddle against a stone on the bottom and gave an exceptionally strong push. I don't know just what happened next. Perhaps my paddle slipped. Del says it did. I know I heard him give a whoop, and I saw the river coming straight up at me. Then it came pouring in over the side, and in about a minute more most of our things were floating downstream, with Del grabbing at them, and me clinging to the upset canoe, trying to drag it ashore.

We camped there. It was a good place, one of the best yet selected. Still, I do not recommend selecting a camp in that way. If it did not turn out well, it might be a poor place to get things dry. One needs to get a good many things dry after a selection like that, especially on a cold day. It was a cold night, too. I dried my under things and put them all on.

"Did you ever sleep in your clothes in the woods?" I have been asked.

I did. I put on every dry thing I had that night, and regretted I had left anything at home.

Chapter Twenty-seven

It is better to let the wild beast run,

And to let the wild bird fly:

Each harbors best in his native nest,

Even as you and I.

Perhaps it was the cold weather that brought us a visitor.
There was a tree directly over our tent, and in the
morning—a sharp sunny morning, with the wind where it
should be, in the west—we noticed on going out that a
peculiar sort of fruit had grown on this tree over night. On
one of the limbs just above the tent was a prickly looking
ball, like a chestnut burr, only black, and about a hundred
times as big. It was a baby porcupine, who perhaps had set
out to see the world on his own account—a sort of prodigal
who had found himself without funds, and helpless, on a
cold night. No doubt he climbed up there to look us over,
with a view of picking out a good place for himself;
possibly with the hope of being invited to breakfast.

Eddie was delighted with our new guest. He declared that
he would take him home alive, and feed him and care for
him, and live happy ever after. He got a pole and shook our
visitor down in a basket, and did a war-dance of joy over
his new possession. He was a cute little fellow—the
"piggypine" (another of Eddie's absurd names)—with

bright little eyes and certain areas of fur, but I didn't fancy him as a pet. He seemed to me rather too much of a cross between a rat and a pin cushion to be a pleasant companion in the intimate relations of one's household. I suspected that if in a perfectly wild state he had been prompted to seek human companionship and the comforts of civilized life, in a domestic atmosphere he would want to sit at the table and sleep with somebody. I did not believe Eddie's affection would survive these familiarities. I knew how surprised and annoyed he might be some night to roll over suddenly on the piggypine and then have to sit up the rest of the night while a surgeon removed the quills. I said that I did not believe in taming wild creatures, and I think the guides were with me in this opinion. I think so because they recited two instances while we were at breakfast. Del's story was of some pet gulls he once owned. He told it in that serious way which convinced me of its truth. Certain phases of the narrative may have impressed me as being humorous, but it was clear they were not so regarded by Del. His manner was that of one who records history. He said:

"One of the children caught two young gulls once, in the lake, and brought them to the house and said they were going to tame them. I didn't think they would live, but they did. You couldn't have killed them without an ax. They got tame right away, and they were all over the house, under foot and into everything, making all kinds of trouble. But that wasn't the worst—the worst was feeding them. It wasn't so bad when they were little, but they grew to beat anything. Then it began to keep us moving to get enough for them to eat. They lived on fish, mostly, and at first the children thought it fun to feed them. They used to bait a little dip net and catch minnows for the gulls, and the gulls got so they would follow anybody that started out with that dip net, calling and squealing like a pair of pigs. But they were worse than pigs. You can fill up a pig and he will go to sleep, but you never could fill up those gulls. By and by the children got tired of trying to do it and gave me the job. I made a big dip net and kept it set day and night, and every few minutes all day and the last thing before bedtime I'd go down and lift out about a pailful of fish for those gulls, and they'd eat until the fish tails stuck out of their mouths, and I wouldn't more than have my back turned before they'd be standing on the shore of the lake, looking down into that dip net and hollering for more. I got so I couldn't do anything but catch fish for those gulls. It was a busy season, too, and besides the minnows were getting scarce along the lake front, so I had to get up early to get enough to feed them and the rest of the family. I said at last that I was through feeding gulls. I told the children that either they'd have to do it, or that the gulls would have to go to work like the rest of the family and fish for themselves. But the children wouldn't do it, nor the gulls, either. Then I said I would take those birds down in the woods and leave them somewhere. I did that. I put them into a basket and shut them in tight and took them five miles down the river and let them loose in a good place where there were plenty of fish. They flew off and I went home. When I got to the house they'd been there three hours, looking at the dip net and squalling, and they ate a pail heaping full of fish, and you could have put both gulls into the pail when they got through. I was going on a long trip with a party next morning, and we took the gulls along. We fed them about a bushel of trout and left them seventeen miles down the river, just before night, and drove home in the dark. I didn't think the gulls would find their way back that time, but they did. They were there before daybreak, fresh and hungry as ever. Then I knew it was no use. The ax was the only thing that would get me out of that mess. The children haven't brought home any wild pets since."

That you see is just unembellished history, and convincing. I regret that I cannot say as much for Charlie's narrative. It is a likely story enough, as such things go, but there are points about it here and there which seem to require confirmation. I am told that it is a story well known and often repeated in Nova Scotia, but even that cannot be accepted as evidence of its entire truth. Being a fish-story it would seem to require something more. This is the tale as Charlie told it.

"Once there was a half-breed Indian," he said, "who had a pet trout named Tommy, which he kept in a barrel. But the trout got pretty big and had to have the water changed a good deal to keep him alive. The Indian was too lazy to do that, and he thought he would teach the trout to live out of water. So he did. He commenced by taking Tommy out of the barrel for a few minutes at a time, pretty often, and then he took him out oftener and kept him out longer, and by and by Tommy got so he could stay out a good while if he was in the wet grass. Then the Indian found he could leave him in the wet grass all night, and pretty soon that trout could live in the shade whether the grass was wet or not. By that time he had got pretty tame, too, and he used to follow the Indian around a good deal, and when the Indian would go out to dig worms for him, Tommy would go along and pick up the worms for himself. The Indian thought everything of that fish, and when Tommy got so he didn't need water at all, but could go anywhere—down the dusty road and stay all day out in the hot sun—you never saw the Indian without his trout. Show people wanted to buy Tommy, but the Indian said he wouldn't sell a fish like that for any money. You'd see him coming to town with

Tommy following along in the road behind, just like a dog, only of course it traveled a good deal like a snake, and most as fast.

"Well, it was pretty sad the way that Indian lost his trout, and it was curious, too. He started for town one day with Tommy coming along behind, as usual. There was a bridge in the road and when the Indian came to it he saw there was a plank off, but he went on over it without thinking. By and by he looked around for Tommy and Tommy wasn't there. He went back a ways and called, but he couldn't see anything of his pet. Then he came to the bridge and saw the hole, and he thought right away that maybe his trout had got in there. So he went to the hole and looked down, and sure enough, there was Tommy, floating on the water, bottom-side up. He'd tumbled through that hole into the brook and drowned."

I think these stories impressed Eddie a good deal. I know they did me. Even if Charlie's story was not pure fact in certain minor details, its moral was none the less evident. I saw clearer than ever that it is not proper to take wild creatures from their native element and make pets of them. Something always happens to them sooner or later. We were through breakfast and Eddie went over to look at his porcupine. He had left it in a basket, well covered with a number of things. He came back right away—looking a little blank I thought.

"He's gone!" he said. "The basket's just as I left it, all covered up, but he isn't in it."

We went over to look. Sure enough, our visitor had set out on new adventures. How he had escaped was a mystery. It didn't matter—both he and Eddie were better off.

But that was a day for animal friends. Where we camped for luncheon, Eddie and I took a walk along the river bank and suddenly found ourselves in a perfect menagerie. We were among a regular group of grown porcupines—we counted five of them—and at the same time there were two blue herons in the water, close by. A step away a pair of partridges ran through the brush and stood looking at us from a fallen log, while an old duck and her young came sailing across the river. We were nearing civilization now, but evidently these creatures were not much harassed. It was like the Garden of Eden before the Fall. It is true the old duck swam away, calling to her brood, when she saw us; the partridges presently hid in the brush, and the blue herons waded a bit further off. But the porcupines went on galumphing around us, and none of the collection seemed much disturbed. During the afternoon we came upon two fishermen, college boys, camping, who told us they had seen some young loons in a nest just above, and Eddie was promptly seized with a desire to possess them.

In fact we left so hastily that Del forgot his extra paddle, and did not discover the loss until we were a half-mile or so upstream. Then he said he would leave me in the canoe to fish and would walk back along the shore. An arm of the river made around an island just there, and it looked like a good place. There seemed to be not much current in the water, and I thought I could manage the canoe in such a spot and fish, too, without much trouble.

It was not as easy as it looked. Any one who has tried to handle a canoe from the front end with one hand and fish with the other will tell you so. I couldn't seem to keep out of the brush along the shore, and I couldn't get near some brush in the middle of the river where I believed there were trout. I was right about the trout being there, too. Eddie proved that when he came up with his canoe. He had plenty of business with big fellows right away. But the fact didn't do me any good. Just when I would get near the lucky place and ready to cast, a twitch in the current or a little puff of wind would get hold of the stern of my craft, which rode up out of the water high and light like a sail, and my flies would land in some bushes along the bank, or hang in a treetop, or do some other silly thing which was entertaining enough to Eddie and his guide, apparently, but which did not amuse me. I never realized before what a crazy thing a canoe can be when you want it to do something out of its regular line of work. A canoe is a good sort of a craft in its place, and I would not wish to go into the woods without one, but it is limited in its gifts, very limited. It can't keep its balance with any degree of certainty when you want to stand up and fish, and it has no sort of notion of staying in one place, unless it's hauled out on the bank. If that canoe had been given the versatility of an ordinary flat-bottomed john-boat I could have got along better than I did. I said as much, and disparaged canoes generally. Eddie declared that he had never heard me swear with such talent and unreserve. He encouraged me by holding up each fish as he caught it and by suggesting that I come over there. He knew very well that I couldn't get there in a thousand years. Whenever I tried to do it that fool of a canoe shot out at a tangent and brought up nowhere. Finally in an effort to reconstruct my rod I dropped a joint of the noibwood overboard, and it went down in about four hundred feet of water. Then I believe I did have a few things to say. I was surprised at my own proficiency. It takes a crucial moment like that to develop real genius. I polished off the situation and I trimmed up the corners. Possibly a touch of sun made me fluent, for it was hot out there, though it was not as hot as a place I told them about, and I dwelt upon its fitness as a permanent abiding place for fishermen in general and for themselves in particular. When I was through and empty I see-sawed over to the bank and waited for Del. I believe I had a feverish hope that they would conclude to take my advice, and that I should never see their canoe and its contents again.

There are always compensations for those who suffer and are meek in spirit. That was the evening I caught the big fish, the fish that Eddie would have given a corner of his immortal soul (if he has a soul, and if it has corners) to have taken. It was just below a big fall—Loon Lake Falls I think they call it—and we were going to camp there. Eddie had taken one side of the pool and I the other and neither of us had caught anything. Eddie was just landing, when something that looked big and important, far down the swift racing current, rose to what I had intended as my last cast. I had the little four-ounce bamboo, but I let the flies go down there—the fly, I mean, for I was casting with one (a big Silver Doctor)—and the King was there, waiting. He took it with a great slop and carried out a long stretch of line. It was a test for the little rod. There had been unkind remarks about the tiny bamboo whip; this was to be justification; a big trout on a long line, in deep, swift water—the combination was perfect. Battle now, ye ruler of the rapids! Show your timber now, thou slender wisp of silk and cane!

But we have had enough of fishing. I shall not dwell upon the details of that contest. I may say, however, that I have never seen Del more excited than during the minutes—few or many, I do not know how few or how many—that it lasted. Every guide wants his canoe to beat, and it was evident from the first that this was the trout of the expedition. I know that Del believed I would never bring that fish to the canoe, and when those heavy rushes came I was harrassed with doubts myself. Then little by little he yielded. When at last he was over in the slower water—out of the main channel—I began to have faith.

So he came in, slowly, slowly, and as he was drawn nearer to the boat, Del seized the net to be ready for him. But I took the net. I had been browbeaten and humiliated and would make my triumph complete. I brought him to the very side of the boat, and I lifted him in. This time the big fish did not get away. We went to where the others had been watching, and I stepped out and tossed him carelessly on the ground, as if it were but an everyday occurrence. Eddie was crushed. I no longer felt bitterness toward him.

I think I shall not give the weight of that fish. As already stated, no one can tell the truth concerning a big fish the first trial, while more than one attempt does not look well in print, and is apt to confuse the reader. Besides, I don't think Eddie's scales were right, anyway.

Chapter Twenty-eight

Then breathe a sigh and a long good-by

To the wilderness to-day,

For back again to the trails of men

Follows the waterway.

Through the Eel-wier—a long and fruitful rapid—we
entered our old first lake, Kedgeemakoogee, this time from
another point. We had made an irregular loop of one
hundred and fifty miles or more—a loop that had extended
far into the remoter wilderness, and had been marked by
what, to me, were hard ventures and vicissitudes, but
which, viewed in the concrete, was recorded in my soul as
a link of pure happiness. We were not to go home
immediately. Kedgeemakoogee is large and there are
entering streams, at the mouth of which the sport at this
season was good. Besides, the teams that were to come for
us would not be due yet for several days, if we had kept
proper account of time.

It was above the Eel-weir, at George's Run, that Eddie had
his first and only success with dry flies. It was just the
place—a slow-moving current between two islands, with
many vicious and hungry trout. They would rise to the
ordinary fly, two at a cast, and when Eddie put on the dry

fly—the artificial miller that sits upright on the water and is an exact imitation of the real article—and let it go floating down, they snapped it up eagerly. It is beautiful fishing—I should really have liked to try it a little. But Eddie had been good to me in so many ways: I hadn't the heart to ask him for one of his precious dry flies.

During our trip across Kedgeemakoogee, Del—inspired perhaps by the fact that we were getting nearer to the walks and wiles of men—gave me some idea of Nova Scotia political economies. He explained the system of government there, the manner of voting and the like. The representation is by districts, of course, similar to our own, and the parties have similar methods of making the vote of these districts count on the right side. In Queens, for instance, where we had been most, if not all, of the time, the voters are very scattering. I had suspected this, for in our one hundred and fifty miles travel we had seen but two natives, and only one of these was believed to have political residence. Del said the district had been gerrymandered a good deal to make the votes count right, and it was plain enough that if this man was the only voter in that much country, and he chasing bears most of the time, they would have to gerrymander around a good deal to keep up with him. Del said that when election time came they would go gunning for that voter over the rocks and through the burnt timber, and would beat up the brush for him as if he were a moose, and valuable. Somehow politics did not seem to belong in this place, but either Del exaggerated, this time, or there is a good deal of it to the individual. I suppose it's well to have it condensed in that way.

We camped that night at Jim Charles's Point, our old first camp, and it was like getting home after long absence. For the time seemed an age since we had left there. It was that. Any new and wonderful experience is long—as long as eternity—whether it be a day or a decade in duration. Next morning, across to the mouth of West River—a place of many fish and a rocky point for our camp, with deep beds of sweet-fern, but no trees. That rocky open was not the best selection for tents. Eddie and his guide had gone up the river a little way when a sudden shower came up, with heavy darkness and quick wind. Del and I were stowing a few things inside that were likely to get wet, when all at once the tents became balloons that were straining at their guy ropes, and then we were bracing hard and clinging fast to the poles to keep everything from sailing into the sky.

It was a savage little squall. It laid the bushes down and turned the lake white in a jiffy. A good thing nobody was out there, under that black sky. Then the wind died and there came a swish of rain—hard rain for a few minutes. After that the sun once more, the fragrance of the fern and the long, sweet afternoon.

Looking at those deep tides of sweet-fern, I had an inspiration. My stretcher had never been over comfortable. I longed to sleep flat. Why not a couch of this aromatic balm? It was dry presently, and spreading the canvas strip smoothly on the ground I covered it with armfuls of the fern, evenly laid. I gathered and heaped it higher until it rose deep and cushiony; then I sank down upon it to perfect bliss.

This was Arcady indeed: a couch as soft and as fragrant as any the gods might have spread by the brooks of Hymettus in that far time when they stole out of Elysium to find joy in the daughters of men. Such a couch Leda might have had when the swan came floating down to bestow celestial motherhood. I buried my face in the odorous mass and vowed that never again would I cramp myself in a canvas trough between two sticks, and I never did. I could not get sweet-fern again, but balsam boughs were plentiful, and properly laid in a manner that all guides know, make a couch that is wide and yielding and full of rest.

Up Little River, whose stones like the proverbial worm, turned when we stepped on them and gave Eddie a hard fall; across Frozen Ocean—a place which justified its name, for it was bitterly cold there and we did nothing but keep the fire going and play pedro (to which end I put on most of my clothes and got into my sleeping-bag)—through another stream and a string of ponds, loitering and exploring until the final day.

It was on one reach of a smaller stream that we found the Beaver Dam—the only one I ever saw, or am likely to see, for the race that builds them is nearly done. I had been walking upstream and fishing some small rapids above the others when I saw what appeared to be a large pool of still water just above. I made my way up there. It was in reality a long stillwater, but a pond rather than a pool. It interested me very much. The dam was unlike any I had ever seen. For one thing, I could not understand why a dam should be in that place, for there was no sign of a sluice or other indication of a log industry; besides, this dam was not composed of logs or of stone, or anything of the sort. It was a woven dam—a dam composed of sticks and brush and rushes and vines, some small trees, and dirt—made without much design, it would seem, but so carefully put together and so firmly bound that no piece of it could work loose or be torn away. I was wondering what people could have put together such a curious and effective thing as that, when Del came up, pushing the canoe. He also was interested when he saw it, but he knew what it was. It was a beaver dam, and they were getting mighty scarce. There was a law against killing the little fellows, but their pelts were worth high prices, and the law did not cover traffic in them. So long as that was the case the beavers would be killed.

I had heard of beaver dams all my life, but somehow I had not thought of their being like this. I had not thought of those little animals being able to construct a piece of engineering that, in a swift place like this, could stand freshet and rot, year after year, and never break away. Del said he had never known one of them to go out. The outlet was in the right place and of the proper size. He showed me some new pieces which the builders had recently put into the work, perhaps because it seemed to be weakening there. He had watched once and had seen some beavers working. They were as intelligent as human beings. They could cut a tree of considerable size, he said, and make it fall in any chosen direction. Then he showed me some pieces of wood from which they had gnawed the sweet bark, and he explained how they cut small trees and sank lengths of them in the water to keep the bark green and fresh for future use. I listened and marveled. I suppose I had read of these things, but they seemed more wonderful when I was face to face with the fact.

The other canoe came up and it was decided to cut a small section out of the dam to let us through. I objected, but was assured that the beavers were not very busy, just now, and would not mind—in fact might rather enjoy—a repair job, which would take them but a brief time.

"They can do it sometime while I'm making a long carry," Charlie said.

But it was no easy matter to cut through. Charlie and Del worked with the ax, and dragged and pulled with their hands. Finally a narrow breach was made, but it would have been about as easy to unload the canoes and lift them over. Half-way up the long hole we came to the lodge—its top rising above the water. Its entrance, of course, was below the surface, but the guides said there is always a hole at the top, for air. It was a well-built house—better, on the whole, than many humans construct.

"They'll be scrambling around, pretty soon," Charlie said, "when they find the water getting lower in their sitting room. Then they'll send out a repair gang. Poor little fellers! Somebody'll likely get 'em before we come again. I know one chap that got seven last year. It's too bad."

Yes, it is too bad. Here is a wonderful race of creatures— ingenious, harmless—a race from which man doubtless derived his early lessons in constructive engineering. Yet Nova Scotia is encouraging their assassination by permitting the traffic in their skins, while she salves her conscience by enacting a law against their open slaughter. Nova Scotia is a worthy province and means well. She protects her moose and, to some extent, her trout. But she ought to do better by the beavers. They are among her most industrious and worthy citizens. Their homes and their industries should be protected. Also, their skins. It can't be done under the present law. You can't put a price on a man's head and keep him from being shot, even if it is against the law. Some fellow will lay for him sure. He will sneak up and shoot him from behind, just as he would sneak up and shoot a beaver, and he will collect his reward in either case, and the law will wink at him. Maybe it would be no special crime to shoot the man. Most likely he deserved it, but the beaver was doing nobody any harm.

Long ago he taught men how to build their houses and their dams, and to save up food and water for a dry time. Even if we no longer need him, he deserves our protection and our tender regard. [6]

Chapter Twenty-nine

Once more, to-night, the woods are white

That lee so dim and far,

Where the wild trout hide and the moose abide

Under the northern star.

Perhaps the brightest spot of that sad period when we were
making ready to leave the woods, with all their comfort,
their peace and their religion, and go back to the harrying
haunts of men, to mingle with the fever and fret of daily
strife, is the memory of a trip to Jeremy's Bay. I don't know
in the least where Jeremy's Bay is, but it is somewhere
within an hour's paddle of Jim Charles's Point, and it is that
hour and the return that sticks with me now.

It was among the last days of June—the most wonderful
season in the north woods. The sun seems never ready to
set there, then, and all the world is made of blues and
greens and the long, lingering tones of evening.

We had early tea in preparation for the sunset fishing. It
was best, Del said, in Jeremy's Bay about that time. So it
was perhaps an hour earlier when we started, the canoes
light.

In any one life there are not many evenings such as that. It is just as well, for I should account it a permanent sadness if they became monotonous. Perhaps they never would. Our course lay between shores—an island on the one hand, the mainland on the other. When we rounded the point, we were met by a breeze blown straight from the sunset—a breath that was wild and fresh and sweet, and billowed the water till it caught every hue and shimmering iridescence that the sky and shores and setting sun could give.

We were eager and rested, for we had done little that day, and the empty canoes slipped like magic into a magical sea of amethyst and emerald gold, the fresh breeze filling us with life and ecstasy until we seemed almost to fly. The eyes could not look easily into the glory ahead, though it was less easy to look away from the enchantment which lay under the sunset. The Kingdom of Ponemah was there, and it was as if we were following Hiawatha to that fair and eternal hunting-ground.

Yet when one did turn, the transformation was almost worth while. The colors were all changed. They were more peaceful, more like reality, less like a harbor of dreams and visions too fair for the eyes of man to look upon. A single glance backward, and then away once more between walls of green, billowing into the sunset—away, away to Jeremy's Bay!

The sun was just on the horizon when we reached there—the water already in shadow near the shore. So deep and vivid were its hues that we seemed to be fishing in dye-stuff. And the breeze went out with the sun, and the painted pool became still, ruffled only where the trout broke water or a bird dipped down to drink.

I will not speak of the fishing there. I have already promised that I would not speak of fishing again. But Jeremy's Bay is a spot that few guides know and few fishermen find. It was our last real fishing, and it was worthy. Then home to camp, between walls of dusk— away, away from Jeremy's Bay—silently slipping under darkening shores—silently, and a little sadly, for our long Day of Joy was closing in—the hour of return drew near.

And postpone it as you will, the final moment must come— the time when the rod must be taken down for good; the leaders stripped and coiled in their box, the fly-book tenderly gone over and the last flies you have used fitted into place and laid away.

One does not go through that final ritual without a little sentiment—a little tugging about the heart. The flies were all new and trim and properly placed when you set out. They were a gay array and you were as proud of them as of a little garden. They are in disarray now. They have an unkempt look. The shells are shredded, the feathers are caked and bitten, the hackle is frazzled and frayed out. Yet you are even more proud of them than in the beginning. Then they were only a promise, fair and beautiful to look upon; now they conjure up pictures of supreme fulfillment—days and moments so firmly set upon the past that they shall not soon fade away. That big Silver Doctor—from which the shell has twice been broken, and the feathers wrapped and rewrapped—that must have been wound with a special blessing, for when all else failed it was a certain lure. The big trout below Loon Lake rose to that fly, and accordingly this battered thing will forever be preserved. This scarlet Breck, with almost every gay feather gone and the silver wrapping replaced with tinfoil—even when it displayed a mere shred of its former glory it proved far more fatal than many a newer fly. How vividly it recalls a certain wild pool of strange, dim lucence where, for me, the trout would take no other lure. And this Montreal—it has become a magic brush that paints a picture of black rocks and dark water, and my first trout taken on a cast. For a hundred years, if I live that long, this crumpled book and these broken, worn-out flies will bring back the clear, wild water and the green shores of a Nova Scotia June, the remoter silences of the deeper forest, the bright camps by twisting pools and tumbling falls, the flash of the leaping trout, the feel of the curved rod and the music of the singing reel.

I shall always recall Eddie, then, and I shall bless him for many things—and forgive him for others. I shall remember Del, too, the Stout, and Charles the Strong, and that they made my camping worth while. I was a trial to them, and they were patient—almost unreasonably so. I am even sorry now for the time that my gun went off and scared Del, though it seemed amusing at the moment. When the wind beats up and down the park, and the trees are bending and cracking with ice; when I know that once more the still places of the North are white and the waters fettered—I shall shut my eyes and see again the ripple and the toss of June, and hear once more the under voices of the falls. And some day I shall return to those far shores, for it is a place to find one's soul.

Yet perhaps I should not leave that statement unqualified, for it depends upon the sort of a soul that is to be found. The north wood does not offer welcome or respond readily to the lover of conventional luxury and the smaller comforts of living. Luxury is there, surely, but it is the luxury that rewards effort, and privation, and toil. It is the comfort of food and warmth and dry clothes after a day of endurance—a day of wet, and dragging weariness, and bitter chill. It is the bliss of reaching, after long, toilsome travel, a place where you can meet the trout—the splendid, full-grown wild trout, in his native home, knowing that you will not find a picnic party on every brook and a fisherman behind every tree. Finally, it is the preciousness of isolation, the remoteness from men who dig up and tear down and destroy, who set whistles to tooting and bells to jingling—who shriek themselves hoarse in the market place and make the world ugly and discordant, and life a short and fevered span in which the soul has a chance to become no more than a feeble and crumpled thing. And if that kind of a soul pleases you, don't go to the woods. It will be only a place of mosquitoes, and general wetness, and discomfort. You won't care for it. You will hate it. But if you are willing to get wet and stay wet—to get cold and stay cold—to be bruised, and scuffed, and bitten—to be hungry and thirsty and to have your muscles strained and sore from unusual taxation: if you will welcome all these things, not once, but many times, for the sake of moments of pure triumph and that larger luxury which comes with the comfort of the camp and the conquest of the wilderness, then go! The wilderness will welcome you, and teach you, and take you to its heart. And you will find your own soul there; and the discovery will be worth while!

FOOTNOTES:

[1] The ordinary New York and New England "half pound trout" will weigh anywhere from four to six ounces. It takes a trout nearly a foot long to weigh half a pound. With each additional inch the weight increases rapidly. A trout thirteen inches in length will weigh about three quarters of a pound. A fourteen-inch trout will weigh a pound. A fifteen-inch trout, in good condition, will weigh one and a half pounds, plump.

[2] When this chapter appeared in The Outing Magazine Frederic Remington wrote as follows:

"My dear Paine: Just read your Outing article on the woods and your speculation on 'why mosquitoes were made,' etc. I know the answer. They were created to aid civilization— otherwise, no man not an idiot would live anywhere else than in the woods."

I am naturally glad to have this word of wisdom from an authority like Remington, but I still think that Providence could have achieved the same result and somehow managed to leave the mosquito out of it.

[3] The publisher wished me to go on with the story at this point. The man referred to above got his experience in Wall Street. He got enough in half a day to keep him in advice for forty-seven years.

[4] Pronounced To-be-at-ic

[5] I believe the best authorities say that one change is enough to take on a camping trip, and maybe it is—for the best authorities.

[6] I have just learned from Eddie that Nova Scotia has recently enacted a new law, adequately protecting the beaver. I shall leave the above, however, as applying to other and less humane districts, wherever located.

Made in the USA
Middletown, DE
01 March 2020

85553905R10099